Recipes From Big Sky Country

A Collection of Montana's Finest Bed & Breakfast Recipes

Montana Bed & Breakfast Association

Winters Publishing
P.O. Box 501
Greensburg, Indiana   47240

800-457-3230
812-663-4948

Cover photo: Jeff Henry
Courtesy of: Paradise Gateway Bed & Breakfast and Guest Cabins
               Emigrant, Montana
               (View from inn and each cabin)

The information about the inns and the recipes were supplied by the inns
themselves. The rate information was current at the time of submission, but
is subject to change. Every effort has been made to assure that the book is
accurate. Neither the editors, the Montana Bed & Breakfast Association, the
individual inns, nor the publisher assume responsibility for any errors,
whether typographical or otherwise.

Library of Congress Control Number 2001093664
ISBN 1-883651-18-2

Preface

This is the second cookbook we have published for the Montana Bed & Breakfast Association. *Recipes From Big Sky Country* offers a wide variety of delicious recipes. The innkeepers invite you to prepare these special dishes in the comfort of your own kitchen.

Many of these recipes are favorites of both the innkeepers and their guests. We are pleased to be able to share them with you.

We hope that you will enjoy preparing the recipes featured in *Recipes From Big Sky Country*. And be sure and plan a visit to Montana soon, to sample your own taste of Big Sky Country!

Rates

We have used the following symbols to represent the price range of the Bed & Breakfast Inns:

$ - $50 or less
$$ - $51 to $75
$$$ - $76 to $100
$$$$ - more than $100

Please call ahead to verify rates and room availability.

CONTENTS

CONTENTS

Appleton Inn

1999 Euclid Avenue • Helena, MT 59601
406-449-7492   800-956-1999
406-449-1261 FAX
Web site: www.appletoninn.com
E-mail: appleton@ixi.net
Innkeepers: Cheryl Boid and Tom Woodall

Relax in the splendor of Helena's Victorian Inn built in 1890 by George Appleton and listed on the National Historic Register. Adorned in original oak and cherry hardwoods, *Appleton Inn* offers five spacious, individually-decorated guest rooms complete with antiques and hand-crafted furnishings, private in-room bath, television, telephone, data ports and all modern comforts you expect from fine Inns. Enjoy afternoon refreshment in the parlor or perennial gardens while planning activities for the evening in this historic city. Return to the *Inn* for a relaxing cup of tea, curl up with a good book or take a long soak in your clawfoot bathtub. After a well-rested sleep, enjoy a delicious full breakfast served on original antique Franciscan Appleware and fine linens, making any morning in Montana special.

Rates: $$$ Includes full breakfast. Children are welcome. Pets allowed with prior approval. Restricted smoking. We accept MasterCard, Visa, Am Ex and Discover.

❖ *Recipes From Appleton Inn* ❖

BANANA CRUMB MUFFINS

1 1/2 cups all-purpose
flour
1 teaspoon baking soda
1 teaspoon baking
powder
1/2 teaspoon salt

3 large ripe bananas,
mashed
3/4 cup sugar
1 egg, lightly beaten
1/3 cup butter or
margarine, melted

Topping:
1/3 cup packed brown
sugar
1 tablespoon flour

1/8 teaspoon ground
cinnamon
1 tablespoon butter or
margarine

Preheat oven to 375°. In large bowl combine the first 4 dry ingredients. In separate bowl mix mashed bananas, sugar, egg and melted butter. Stir banana mixture into dry ingredients until just moistened. Fill muffin cups 2/3 full. Combine first 3 topping ingredients. Cut in butter until crumbly. Sprinkle over muffins. Bake for 18 to 20 minutes. Cool in pan for 10 minutes before removing to a wire rack. Makes 1 dozen muffins.

HAM & CHEESE QUICHE

16 slices bread, with
crusts trimmed
1 pound ham, cubed
8 ounces Swiss cheese
8 ounces cheddar
cheese

3 cups milk
6 eggs
1/2 teaspoon onion salt
1 1/2 cups Corn Flakes
cereal, crushed
1/4 cup melted butter

Place 8 bread slices in 9" x 13" baking pan. Layer half of the ham and half of the cheeses. Place remaining 8 bread slices on top. Layer remaining ham and cheeses. Combine milk, eggs and onion salt in bowl; mix well. Pour over layered mixture. Refrigerate overnight. Remove from refrigerator 30 minutes before baking. Preheat oven to 350°. Combine crushed Corn Flakes and margarine. Sprinkle on top. Bake for 40 minutes. Makes 12 servings.

ORANGE POPPY TEA BREAD

1 cup sour cream
3/4 cup sugar
1/2 cup butter or
  margarine, softened
2 large eggs
1 tablespoon poppy seeds
1 tablespoon grated
  orange rind

2 tablespoons orange
  juice
2 cups flour
1 teaspoon baking
  powder
1 teaspoon baking
  soda
1/2 teaspoon salt

Preheat oven to 325°. Grease a 9" x 5" loaf pan. In large bowl beat sour cream, sugar and butter until light and fluffy. Beat in eggs, poppy seeds, orange rind and orange juice until mixed well. In separate bowl mix flour, baking powder, baking soda and salt. Add to large bowl, mixing at low speed and scraping sides until combined. Pour into loaf pan and bake for 50 to 55 minutes until the center springs back. Cool on rack. Wrap with plastic wrap and let stand overnight. Makes 1 loaf.

SUNRISE SAUSAGE CASSEROLE

1 pound bulk sausage,
  (such as Jimmy Dean)
  browned & drained
1/2 cup chopped onion
12 eggs
1 1/2 cups milk
1 teaspoon salt
1/2 teaspoon pepper
1 teaspoon parsley

1/2 teaspoon thyme
1/4 teaspoon dill weed
1 (16-ounce) pkg. frozen
  hashbrown potatoes,
  cubed & thawed
1 cup shredded cheddar
  cheese
1/2 cup chopped green
  pepper

Preheat oven to 350°. In skillet cook sausage and onion. Set aside. Beat eggs and milk in large bowl. Add salt, pepper, parsley, thyme and dill. Stir in hashbrowns, cheese, green pepper, sausage and onions. Transfer to a 9" x 13" x 2" baking dish. Bake uncovered, for 35 to 45 minutes or until a knife inserted near the center comes out clean. Makes 6 - 8 servings.

TOASTED ALMOND FRENCH TOAST

1/4 cup sliced unblanched
  almonds
3 large eggs
1 cup milk
2 tablespoons flour
1/2 teaspoon baking
  powder

1/8 teaspoon salt
1 teaspoon vanilla
  extract
1/2 teaspoon almond
  extract
6 slices French bread,
  cut 1/2" thick

Preheat oven to 350°. Spread almonds on a baking sheet and toast in the oven for 10 minutes, until lightly browned and fragrant. Remove to plate and set aside to cool. In medium bowl whisk together eggs, milk, flour, baking powder, salt, vanilla and almond extracts. Dip both sides of bread into egg mixture and place in shallow pan. Pour remaining mixture over bread slices and allow to soak for 1 hour, or cover and refrigerate overnight. Preheat griddle. Spray with cooking spray. Cook French toast until well-browned, for about 3 to 5 minutes. Turn over and cook. Place French toast on plate, sprinkle with powdered sugar and garnish with almonds. Serve with warm syrup and fresh fruit. Makes 3 servings.

WALNUT REFRIGERATOR MUFFINS

2 cups all-purpose flour
Dash of salt
1/2 teaspoon baking
  soda
1/2 cup shortening

1 egg
1 cup packed light
  brown sugar
1 cup milk
1/2 cup walnuts, chopped

Preheat oven to 350°. Blend flour, salt and baking soda. Set aside. In large mixing bowl cream shortening, egg and brown sugar until light and fluffy. Add dry ingredients and milk alternately to creamed mixture, beating well after each addition. Stir in walnuts. Chill for 24 hours or longer. Spoon batter into muffin cups and bake for 20 minutes. Makes 1 dozen muffins.

The Barrister Bed & Breakfast

416 North Ewing Street • Helena, MT 59601
406-443-7330   800-823-1148
406-442-7964 FAX
Web site: www.wtp.net/go/montana/sites/barrister.html
E-mail: barister@rcisys.net
Innkeepers: Nick Jacques and Jacquie Bennett

The Barrister is an elegant 1880 Victorian three-story mansion listed on the National Register of Historic Places. It is located in the center of Helena, adjacent to the magnificent St. Helena Cathedral and walking distance to downtown with fine restaurants, shops and galleries. The mansion features six ornate fireplaces, original stained glass windows, high ceilings and carved staircases. 5 guest rooms on the second floor are exquisitely decorated, have private baths and feature queen size turn of the century replica beds. The first floor common area boasts a formal dining room, grand piano and guitar in the parlor, enclosed sun porch with ice cream parlor tables, business center/game room, office with computer and office equipment, large outside porch and large yard with waterfall for guests' use and enjoyment. Airport shuttle and evening refreshments are offered.

Rates: $$$ Includes full breakfast. Children are welcome.
Pets allowed. Restricted smoking. We accept MasterCard, Visa,
Am Ex and Discover.

STUFFED APPLE-BRANDY FRENCH TOAST

Topping:

1/2 cup sugar
2 teaspoons cinnamon

1/2 teaspoon
  nutmeg

Toast:

1 loaf day-old French
  bread, sliced 1" thick
2 (8-ounce) pkgs. cream
  cheese, softened
4 sliced Granny Smith
  apples

12 eggs
2 cups 2% milk
1/2 cup brandy
1 tablespoon vanilla
4 tablespoons sugar

Combine Topping ingredients and set aside. Slice French bread into 1" slices and arrange to cover a 9" x 13" pan coated with vegetable spray. Spread cream cheese over bread and add a layer of sliced apples. Add half of the Topping over apples. Add a second layer of bread and apples. Mix eggs, milk, brandy, vanilla and sugar. Beat lightly and pour over bread. Spread with remaining Topping. Bake at 400° for 30 minutes. Serve with Cinnamon Syrup (see recipe below).

CINNAMON SYRUP

1 cup white corn syrup
1 cup sugar
1/4 cup water

1/2 teaspoon ground
  cinnamon
1/2 cup evaporated milk

Mix all ingredients except evaporated milk in a saucepan and bring to boil. Boil for 2 minutes. Let cool for 5 minutes and add evaporated milk. Serve warm. Makes 12 servings. Serve over Stuffed Apple-Brandy French Toast (see recipe above).

Beardance Inn & Cabins

135 Bay Drive • Bigfork, MT
Send mail to: PMB 120, 439 Grand Avenue • Bigfork, MT 59911
406-837-4551   888-443-2699
E-mail: beardanc@digisys.net
Innkeeper: Clara Morehouse

Feel Montana's Magic. We offer accommodations in a 60-year-old log home with a main lodge and 6 little homestead-style cabins. Repairs and renovations carefully preserve the original charm. Prices include a hearty breakfast with an entree, local seasonal fruit and home-baked goods. You will dine in the main lodge overlooking the waters of Bigfork Bay (where the Swan River flows into Flathead Lake). For your entertainment, osprey fish and play along the shoreline. Enjoy the main lodge fireplace, boat docks, smoke-free interiors, BBQ's, picnic tables, Flathead Lake and walking to the village. Bigfork village provides great summer theater, world-class restaurants, unique shops and boutiques and the galleries of many of today's most talented Western artists. Open year-round for reunions, retreats, small weddings, holiday packages.

Rates: $$$ - $$$$ Includes full breakfast. Children are welcome.
No pets, please. Restricted smoking (outside only).

BEARDANCE GRANOLA

1 cup butter
1/4 cup honey
1/4 cup + 2 tablespoons
   real maple syrup
1 pound old-fashioned
   rolled oats
1 cup coarsely chopped
   almonds
1 cup coarsely chopped
   pecans

1 1/2 teaspoons ground
   cinnamon
1/2 teaspoon fresh
   grated nutmeg
Zest grated from
   2 oranges
1 cup toasted
   coconut (opt.)
Seeds or dried
   fruits (opt.)

Melt butter, honey and maple syrup together. In a large bowl mix remaining ingredients. Pour syrup over dry mixture and stir to blend. Pack granola down on buttered cookie pan. Bake at 350° for 20 to 30 minutes until golden brown and it sticks together. When granola is cooled, place in mixing bowl and we add coconut. (May add seeds or dried fruits.) Freezes well in ziplock bags. Store airtight. Makes 2 quarts granola.

SALMON QUICHE

1 (10") pie shell, baked
1 small salmon filet
   (approximately 1 1/2
   cups broken pieces)
1/2 - 3/4 cup broccoli
   flowerets
1/2 cup chopped white
   onions
1/2 cup sweet peppers
   (mixed colors)

1 tablespoon olive oil
4 eggs, beaten
3/4 cup half and half
   cream
1 1/4 cups milk
1 tablespoon fresh herbs
   (tarragon or oregano)
Salt & pepper, to taste
1/2 pound grated
   Swiss cheese

Grill salmon filet until lightly done. Just before filling, prebake pie crust at 375° for 10 minutes. Steam broccoli al dente. Sauté onions and peppers together in olive oil. Layer onions and peppers, broccoli and salmon pieces in slightly baked pie crust. Beat together eggs, half and half cream, milk, herbs, salt and pepper. Pour egg mix over all. Top with Swiss cheese. Bake at 375° for 30 to 40 minutes until set. (Knife in center comes out clean.) Let stand for 10 minutes before slicing. Makes 8 - 10 servings.

Big Creek Pines Bed & Breakfast

2986 Highway 93 North • Stevensville, MT 59870
406-642-6475   888-300-6475
Web site: www.bigcreekpines.com
E-mail: bcp1@cybernet1.com
Innkeepers: Rosemary and Joe Beason

Welcome! As you enter the door of *Big Creek Pines*, you feel a sense of home. Guests love how treasured family mementos have been used in decorating this warm, friendly bed and breakfast. Gorgeous views of the Bitterroot and Sapphire Mountains from every window. Four spacious guest rooms, each with private in-room bath, fresh flowers and window seats, to enjoy that early morning cup of coffee, read a magazine or just to enjoy the views overlooking the creek, meadow and mountains. A beautifully-set candlelit table awaits you for breakfast, where you are served fresh fruit juice smoothies, a variety of delectable entrees and freshly baked breads and pastries. We are located on the Lewis and Clark Trail, just 27 miles south of Missoula, in historic Stevensville, where Montana began. Be sure to bring your hiking boots, fishing rods, binoculars and camera. Please check out our web site.

Rates: $$$ Includes full breakfast. No pets, please. Restricted smoking. We accept MasterCard and Visa.

AEBELSKIVERS

1 cup flour
1/8 teaspoon salt
1 tablespoon sugar
1 teaspoon baking powder
1/4 teaspoon baking soda
1/4 teaspoon cardamom

1 cup buttermilk
1/4 teaspoon vanilla
2 teaspoons melted butter
2 eggs, separated (use 1 yolk, discard 1 yolk)

Sift together dry ingredients. Blend buttermilk, vanilla, melted butter and 1 egg yolk. Add to flour mixture. Beat 2 egg whites until stiff; fold into mixture. Place aebelskiver pan over low heat and add small amount of melted butter to each cup. Pour batter into holes, filling 3/4 full. Cook over low heat and turn quickly with ice pick or knitting needle, when cakes begin to brown around edges. Serve hot with apple syrup or a mandarin orange sauce. Makes 2 servings.

LEMON & OLIVE CAVIAR

2 cups seedless black olives
1 1/2 tablespoons fresh garlic
1 teaspoon freshly ground black pepper
1 1/2 teaspoons fine lemon zest

2 tablespoons fresh lemon juice
2 tablespoons chopped onion
2 1/2 tablespoons good olive oil
1 1/2 tablespoons Worcestershire sauce

Add all ingredients into a food processor and process just to a fine mixture. Chill and serve with baguettes or crackers. Makes 6 - 8 servings.

❖ *Recipes From Big Creek Pines Bed & Breakfast*

OMELET SOUFFLÉ
WITH RASPBERRY SAUCE

Omelet Soufflé:
3 tablespoons flour
1 tablespoon orange or
 lemon zest
12 eggs, separated
2 tablespoons sugar

Raspberry Sauce:
1 (10-ounce) pkg. frozen
 & thawed raspberries,
 in light syrup
 (reserve juice)
1 teaspoon cornstarch

For Raspberry Sauce: Press raspberries through sieve and reserve juice. In small saucepan add cornstarch, then gradually add raspberry juice, stirring until blended. Cook, stirring constantly, until thickened. For Soufflé: Combine flour, orange zest and egg yolks. Combine egg whites and sugar, whipping until stiff. Gently fold beaten whites into the egg yolks mixture. Place a small amount of sauce in the bottom of each of eight ramekins. Lightly spoon soufflé mixture on top of sauce, dividing equally. Bake at 375° for 10 minutes or until lightly browned and set. To serve, spoon on sauce and garnish with fresh raspberries. Makes 8 servings.

ORANGE YOGURT SAUCE
FOR FRESH FRUIT

1 cup fat-free vanilla
 yogurt
1 teaspoon orange zest

1/4 cup frozen orange
 juice concentrate,
 undiluted

Combine all ingredients until well blended. Cover and refrigerate until serving time. Best if prepared a couple of hours prior to serving. Serve over fresh fruit of your choice.

POTATO MADELINES

3 cups mashed potatoes
1/2 cup cornmeal
1/2 cup softened butter
1/4 cup milk
1/4 teaspoon salt

1/8 teaspoon white pepper
1 whole egg, plus
1 egg yolk
2 tablespoons chopped
fresh chives

Combine all ingredients until well mixed. Spoon mixture into well-greased madeline pans. Bake at 500° for 10 to 12 minutes or until golden brown. Makes approximately 24 madelines.

WHEAT-FREE RICE MUFFINS

2 cups rice flour
2 teaspoons baking
powder
1/2 cup sugar
1 teaspoon salt
1 egg

1 1/2 cups milk
2 tablespoons butter or
margarine, melted
Dried cranberries or
raisins (opt.)
Cinnamon/sugar mixture

Sift dry ingredients. Combine egg, milk and melted butter. Add to dry ingredients. Stir ingredients just enough to combine. Gently add fruit, if desired. Fill muffin cups 2/3 full. Sprinkle with mixture of cinnamon and sugar. Bake at 400° for approximately 25 minutes. Makes 12 muffins.

Thanks Jenn for choosing The Big Horn when in the Philipsburg Area! Jimmy

Big Horn Bed & Breakfast

31 Lower Rock Creek Road • Philipsburg, MT 59858
406-859-3109 (Phone & FAX)
Web site: bighornmontana.com
E-mail: ~~bighornbnb~~@blackfoot.net   *bg hrn bNb*
Innkeepers: Virginia and Jerry Gallagher

The Big Horn extends a hearty welcome to all our guests. Nestled in a mountain setting on a blue-ribbon trout stream 15 miles west of Philipsburg, our log home features a large living and dining area with fireplace and decks. We have two beautiful guest rooms - Devon and Ashley - with a shared bath. And we use only environmentally friendly products by Melaleuca for your comfort and safety. If you're searching for serene mountain beauty with a touch of natural elegance, where big horn sheep roam the hills and eagles soar the Montana skies to the music of bluebirds and other wildlife, we have a place for you. Why Rock Creek? It's beautiful, it's peaceful and the fishing is great.

Rates: $$ Includes full breakfast. Children are welcome. No pets, please. Restricted smoking. We accept MasterCard and Visa.

BERRY FRENCH TOAST COBBLER

4 eggs
1/2 cup half & half cream
1 teaspoon vanilla
1 teaspoon baking powder
10 slices French toast
2 tablespoons melted
  butter

4 cups mixed berries
  (raspberries, blueberries
  & blackberries)
1/2 cup sugar
1 teaspoon cornstarch
1 teaspoon cinnamon
1 tablespoon butter

Using medium bowl beat eggs, half & half, vanilla and baking powder. Pour into a 9" x 13" baking dish. Add bread slices. Cover and chill overnight. Next morning combine melted butter, berries, sugar, cornstarch and cinnamon. Pour into a greased 9" x 13" baking dish. Put bread slices over berries & top with remaining 1 tablespoon butter. Bake uncovered, at 400° for approximately 30 minutes until bubbly & golden. Serve hot with hot berry syrup. Makes 6 servings.

FOUR-DAY MAKE AHEAD
SOUR CREAM FUDGE TORTE

Fudge Torte:
1 box Pillsbury Plus
  devil's food cake mix
3 eggs
1 cup water
1/2 cup oil

Sour Cream Filling:
2 cups dairy sour cream
1 cup sugar
3 cups coconut
3 cups non-dairy
  whipped topping

Heat oven to 350°. Grease and flour two 8" cake pans. In large bowl blend ingredients for Fudge Torte at low speed until moistened. Beat for 2 minutes at highest speed. Pour into pans. Bake for 30 to 40 minutes or until toothpick comes out clean. Cool cake in pans on cooling rack for 15 minutes. Remove from pans and cool completely. Split each layer in half, forming 4 layers. Fill and frost with Sour Cream Filling: In large bowl combine sour cream, sugar and coconut. Gently fold in whipped topping. Use to fill between layers and to frost sides and top of Torte. Store covered in refrigerator.

PASTIES

1 pound pasty meat
(coarsely ground
hamburger)
4 cups diced potatoes
1 large onion, chopped
1 1/2 teaspoons salt

1/2 teaspoon black pepper
1 cup thick gravy or
substitute undiluted
cream of mushroom
or celery soup

Pie Crust:
3 cups enriched flour
2 teaspoons baking
powder

1 tablespoon sugar
1 cup lard
About 1/2 cup <u>cold</u>
water

Mix meat, potatoes, onion, salt, pepper, and gravy or soup together. Make pie crust: Mix dry ingredients. Then add lard and blend until mixture is like coarse meal. Add cold water. Shape into a ball and roll out on floured board. Using a saucer for a pattern, cut out six circles. Put about 1/4 cup meat mixture on one-half of each circle. Fold over, and using a fork dipped in flour, press down edges. Prick several small holes in top of crust. Bake at 350° for 45 minutes to an hour. Serve with additional gravy, cole slaw, pickled beets, beverage and sheet cake to make a balanced and attractive meal. Note: May substitute cubed leftover roast or venison, elk or moose.

REFRIGERATOR MUFFINS

2 cups oatmeal
2 cups Shredded Wheat
2 cups 100% Bran
2 cups boiling water
1 heaping cup shortening

4 eggs
1 teaspoon salt
5 teaspoons baking soda
1 quart buttermilk
5 cups flour

Soak oatmeal, Shredded Wheat and 100% Bran with water. While still warm, add shortening. Add remaining ingredients. Keep this refrigerated in an airtight container. You can add dates, raisins or any type of fruit, if desired. When ready to prepare muffins, bake at 375° for 18 minutes.

Recipes From Big Horn Bed & Breakfast

SOURDOUGH HOTCAKES

Sourdough Starter:
2 cups flour

2 cups warm water
1 pkg. dry yeast

Hotcakes:
4 eggs
2 teaspoons baking
  soda

1/2 teaspoon salt
2 tablespoons sugar
4 tablespoons melted fat

Stir Sourdough Starter ingredients together well. Place in a warm place or closed cupboard overnight. In the morning put 1/2 cup starter in a scalded pint jar with a tight cover and store in refrigerator for future use. For Hotcakes: To remaining Sourdough Starter batter (which will be covered with air bubbles and have a pleasant, yeasty odor) add eggs, baking soda, salt and sugar. Beat with a fork and blend all ingredients. Add melted fat. Bake on a hot griddle. Turn once, and serve with syrup or jelly. Makes hotcakes for 6 people.

SOURDOUGH MUFFINS

Sourdough Starter:
2 cups flour

2 cups warm water
1 pkg. dry yeast

Muffins:
1 1/2 cups whole
  wheat flour
1/2 cup sugar
1 teaspoon salt
1/4 cup nonfat dry milk

1 teaspoon baking
  soda
1 or 2 eggs
1/2 cup melted fat
1 cup raisins (opt.)

The Sourdough Starter should be made slightly thicker than for Hotcakes, then let stand in a warm place overnight. In the morning remove 1/2 cup batter and refrigerate. Use remaining starter batter for Muffins. Sift dry ingredients for Muffins into a bowl. Make a well in the center. To remaining Sourdough Starter batter (which will be covered with air bubbles and have a pleasant, yeasty odor) add egg(s) and melted fat. Add this mixture to the dry ingredients. Stir only enough to moisten the flour. Add raisins, if desired. Fill greased muffin tins 3/4 full. Bake at 375° for 30 to 35 minutes. Makes 20 small or 12 large muffins.

Bonnie's Bed & Breakfast

265 Lake Blaine Road • Kalispell, MT 59901
406-755-3776   800-755-3778
406-752-5544 FAX
Web site: www.wtp.net/go/montana/sites/bonnie.html
E-mail: bonnie@in-tch.com
Innkeepers: Leonard and Bonnie Boles

We appreciate the opportunity to tell you about *Bonnie's Bed & Breakfast*! We live about seven miles outside Kalispell in a rural setting. However, a service station/convenience store and a nice restaurant are only minutes away. 30 minutes from Glacier National Park and 20 minutes from Flathead Lake, with a nine-hole golf course about a block away! The Big Sky Room (Honeymoon Suite) has an open beam ceiling, windows along one wall, a queen size, four poster bed, telephone and TV. Bath has a double sink vanity and a shower/jetted tub for your relaxation. We also offer the Blaine Room (king size bed), Columbian Room, Alpine Room, and Garden Room. Rooms have queen size beds, TV's and telephones. A "Great Room" offers fireplace, TV/VCR, movies and reading material. We serve a full breakfast, starting with fruit, in season. We often serve raspberries and ice cream, with raspberries from our own large raspberry patch!

Rates: $$$ - $$$$ Includes full breakfast. Children are welcome.
No pets, please. Restricted smoking. We accept
MasterCard and Visa.

BAKED OATMEAL

2 cups old-fashioned oats
1/2 teaspoon salt
1/2 cup sugar (can use
 1/4 cup sugar)
1 teaspoon baking
 powder

1/2 cup melted butter
1 cup milk (more, if
 needed*)
1 egg
1/2 teaspoon
 cinnamon (opt.)

Mix all ingredients together. Let stand for 5 or 6 minutes. *If too thick, add more milk. Pour into square 8" x 8" baking dish. Bake at 350° for 30 minutes or until knife comes out clean. For a different flavor, add chopped pecans, dates or raisins. Makes 4 - 6 servings.

BREAKFAST SKILLET

1 (12-ounce) pkg. pork
 sausage links
5 medium apples, peeled
 & quartered (about
 1 1/4 pounds)

3 tablespoons brown
 sugar
1 tablespoon lemon
 juice
1/8 teaspoon salt

In a 10" skillet over medium-high heat, cook sausages for 10 minutes, turning occasionally. Drain. Add apple wedges. Sprinkle with brown sugar, lemon juice and salt. Cover and cook over medium heat for 10 to 15 minutes, or until apples are tender and sausages are fully cooked. Makes 6 servings.

COCONUT FRUIT DIP

1 (8-ounce) can crushed unsweetened pineapple, undrained
3/4 cup skim milk
1/2 cup nonfat sour cream

1 (3.4 ounce) box instant coconut cream pudding mix
Fresh pineapple, grapes, strawberries or any other fruit combination

In a blender combine the first four ingredients; cover and process for 1 minute or until smooth. Serve with fruit. Store in refrigerator. Makes 2 cups of fruit dip.

FRESH APPLE BREAD

1 cup sugar
1/2 cup shortening
2 eggs
1 or 2 cups apple, peeled & grated
2 cups flour
1/2 teaspoon baking soda

1 teaspoon baking powder
1/2 teaspoon vanilla
1 1/2 tablespoons buttermilk or sour milk
1 cup nuts, chopped (pecans are best!)

<u>Topping</u>:
3 tablespoons sugar
1 tablespoon cinnamon

2/3 tablespoon flour
Soft butter, as needed

Cream sugar and shortening. Add eggs and apple. Mix in dry ingredients, then vanilla, buttermilk and nuts. Pour into loaf pan. Sprinkle top with topping mixture. Bake at 350° for about 50 minutes. Makes 1 loaf.

GOOD COMPANY EGGS

1/2 pound grated
  Swiss cheese
1 cup heavy cream
1/2 teaspoon salt
Dash of pepper

1 1/2 teaspoons
  Coleman's Best
  dry mustard
12 eggs, lightly
  beaten

Butter a glass baking pan. (I use a glass pie plate.) Cover bottom of pan with grated cheese. Mix cream with seasonings. Pour half of the cream over the cheese. Add eggs, lightly beaten. Pour on the rest of the cream. Bake at 325° for 30 minutes. Makes 4 - 6 servings.

MUNCHIES

1 (10-ounce) pkg.
  mini-pretzels
5 cups Cheerios cereal
5 cups Corn Chex cereal
2 cups salted peanuts

1 large bag of M&M's
2 (12-ounce) pkgs.
  white chocolate chips
3 tablespoons
  vegetable oil

In a large bowl combine first five ingredients; set aside. In a microwave safe bowl heat chips and oil on medium or high for 2 minutes; stir. Microwave on high for 10 seconds, stir until smooth. Pour over mixture and mix well. Spread onto wax paper-lined cookie sheets. Cool - break apart and store in an air-tight container. Makes 5 quarts of snack.

Bungalow Bed & Breakfast

2020 Highway 287 - P.O. Box 168 • Wolf Creek, MT 59648
406-235-4276   888-286-4250
E-mail: bngalow@aol.com
Innkeeper: Pat O'Connell Anderson

The Bungalow is a red cedar log lodge built in 1911 by early day Montana entrepreneur, C. B. Power. The architect, Robert Reamer, also built lodges in Yellowstone Park. It is on the National Register of Historic Places and has been in the innkeeper's family since 1946. Located under a magnificent rock reef not far from beautiful Wolf Creek Canyon and I-15, it is close to blue ribbon fly fishing on the Missouri and Dearborn Rivers, as well as a scenic boat trip along the Lewis and Clark Trail. Enjoy the quiet of nature and watch the deer meander through the yard or gaze up at the eagles soaring overhead. Spend an enjoyable evening in the great room in front of the massive stone fireplace and wake to a full gourmet breakfast served in the formal dining room. We offer four guest rooms. Conveniently located off scenic Highway 287. Enjoy great Western hospitality!

Rates: $$$ Includes full breakfast. Children are welcome.
No pets, please. Restricted smoking.

Recipes From Bungalow Bed & Breakfast

BANANA PECAN PANCAKES WITH CRANBERRY ORANGE SAUCE

Pancake Batter:
2 cups honey whole
  wheat pancake mix
1 3/4 - 2 cups water
1 large, very ripe
  banana, mashed
1 1/2 teaspoons cinnamon
1/2 cup chopped pecans
Pecan halves, for garnish

Cranberry Orange Sauce:
1 cup sugar
3/4 cup water
3 cups fresh or frozen
  cranberries
3/4 cup orange juice
2 teaspoons freshly
  grated orange peel
1 teaspoon cinnamon

For Pancake Batter: Mix all ingredients together, adding enough water to make the right consistency for griddle. Cook until lightly browned on both sides. Serve with a dollop of Cranberry Orange Sauce and garnish with pecan halves. For Sauce: Mix sugar and water and heat to boiling. Add cranberries, orange juice, orange peel and cinnamon. Return to boil and simmer until all berries are popped. Crush to make a thicker sauce, or puree in food processor to make a smooth sauce.

BERRY-PEACH COBBLER

6 - 8 ripe peaches,
  peeled & sliced
1 cup raspberries
1 cup blueberries
2 cups sugar
2 cups flour

2 teaspoons baking
  powder
2 eggs
2 tablespoons melted
  butter
1/2 cup milk

Place fruit in a 9" x 13" baking pan that has been sprayed with Pam spray. Mix together sugar, flour and baking powder. Stir in eggs, melted butter and milk. Spread over fruit mixture. Bake at 350° for 45 to 60 minutes, until topping is cooked through. This might take a little longer, depending upon juice level of fruit. Serve with vanilla ice cream or a little half and half. Best while still warm!

Recipes From Bungalow Bed & Breakfast

CHEVRE ROUNDS

1 baguette, sliced into
  1/4" thick rounds
Olive oil,
  as needed

1 pkg. chevre
  (goat cheese)
1 can sun-ripened
  tomatoes, in oil

Place bread rounds on baking sheet. Brush with olive oil. Top each with 1/2 - 1 teaspoon cheese, and place a piece of tomato on each. You may want to cut the larger pieces of tomato in half. Place under broiler briefly just to toast edges of bread. Be careful not to burn the tomatoes. This recipe makes a quick appetizer.

CURRIED CHICKEN SALAD

5 pounds chicken breasts,
  simmered in broth
1 1/2 cups chopped
  celery
1 tart apple, diced
1 cup green grapes

1 - 1 1/2 cups Miracle
  Whip (no substitutes)
2 - 4 teaspoons curry
  powder
1/2 cup chopped
  cashews

Cook chicken breasts in broth until done, cool and chop into about 1/2" pieces. Add celery, apple and grapes. Mix well. Add Miracle Whip. Stir in curry powder, to taste, and add cashews. Chill. Makes 6 - 8 servings.

❖ *Recipes From Bungalow Bed & Breakfast* ❖

FROZEN HUCKLEBERRY MUFFINS

1 cup butter or
 margarine, softened
2 cups sugar
4 eggs, slightly beaten
2 teaspoons vanilla
1/2 teaspoon salt

4 teaspoons baking
 powder
4 cups flour
1 cup milk
2 cups frozen
 huckleberries

Topping:
2 tablespoons sugar

1 teaspoon nutmeg

Cream margarine and 2 cups sugar. Add eggs and vanilla. Mix in salt, baking powder, flour and milk. Carefully fold in huckleberries. Spoon into 18 muffin cups. Sprinkle top with mixture of 2 tablespoons sugar and nutmeg. Bake at 375° for 25 to 30 minutes.

GINGERSNAPS

1 cup brown sugar
3/4 cup shortening
1 egg
2 cups flour
2 teaspoons baking soda

1/2 teaspoon salt
1 teaspoon cinnamon
2 teaspoons ginger
3/4 teaspoon cloves
Granulated sugar

Mix together all ingredients except granulated sugar. Let batter stand in refrigerator for at least 3 hours for flavors to blend. (Overnight is best.) Roll into 1" balls, roll dough balls in granulated sugar and place 2" apart on ungreased cookie sheet. Bake at 350° for 12 to 15 minutes. Wonderful with fresh lemonade!

 *Recipes From Bungalow Bed & Breakfast*

GRILLED PORK LOIN CHOPS
WITH MANGO SALSA

6 lean boneless thick
   pork loin chops
Citrus marinade (opt.)
2 ripe mangoes, chopped
1 red onion, chopped

1/4+ cup balsamic
   vinegar
1 tablespoon lime
   juice
1 tablespoon honey

If desired, marinate pork chops in a citrus marinade for 30 to 60 minutes. Grill on barbecue until juices run clear. For Mango Salsa: Combine mangoes, onion, vinegar, lime juice and honey. Garnish chops with salsa or serve it on the side.

MEATBALLS IN RED WINE SAUCE

Meatballs:
1 1/2 pounds extra lean
   ground beef
1/2 cup Corn Flake
   crumbs
1 small grated sweet
   onion
2 teaspoons cornstarch
1 teaspoon salt

1 egg, beaten
2 tablespoons
   Worcestershire sauce
1/3 cup ketchup
2 tablespoons sweet
   pickle relish
1 (5-ounce) can
   evaporated milk

Red Wine Sauce:
2 1/4 tablespoons
   cornstarch
2 beef bouillon cubes
1 cup water

3/4 cup dark red, dry
   wine (Burgandy, Merlot
   or Cabernet)
Salt & pepper, to taste

Mix all meatball ingredients together well. Form into balls - small ones for appetizers or larger ones for a main dish. Bake at 400° for about 15 minutes. Serve with Red Wine Sauce or gravy of your choice. For Sauce: Combine all ingredients and simmer, stirring constantly, over medium heat until thick. Pour over meatballs in chafing dish.

MELON COMPOTE

Honeydew, cantaloupe, and/or watermelon, cubed or scooped into melon balls

Triple sec or other citrus fruit liqueur, to taste

Cube or melon ball a variety of melons. Sprinkle fruit lightly with Triple sec or another citrus fruit liqueur, and stir gently. Serve!

OATMEAL CAKE

1 1/4 cups boiling water
1 cup quick oats
1/2 cup margarine
1 cup white sugar
1 cup brown sugar

2 eggs
1 1/2 cups flour
2 teaspoons cinnamon
1 teaspoon baking soda
1 teaspoon salt

Icing:
1 cup brown sugar
1/2 cup margarine

2/3 cup evaporated milk
1 cup coconut
1 cup chopped pecans

Combine boiling water, oats and margarine in small saucepan and cover. Let stand for 20 minutes. Meanwhile, mix remaining cake ingredients. Blend in oatmeal mixture. Pour into a greased and floured 9" x 13" pan. Bake at 350° for 35 minutes. While cake is baking, combine icing ingredients in saucepan over medium-high heat, bringing to a boil. When cake is done, remove from oven and turn on broiler. Spread hot icing over cake and put under broiler for 5 to 10 minutes, until it bubbles and starts to caramelize. Be careful not to burn it. Enjoy! This is an old family favorite!

ORANGE ROLLS

1 cup milk, scalded
1 teaspoon salt
4 tablespoons butter
or margarine
4 tablespoons sugar
2 packages yeast
1/2 cup warm water
1 egg, slightly beaten
4 1/2 cups flour

Orange Filling:
1/2 cup white sugar
1/2 cup brown
sugar
2 teaspoons grated
orange rind
1/4 cup orange juice
concentrate

Scald milk. While cooling, add salt, butter or margarine and 4 tablespoons sugar. Cool to lukewarm. Dissolve yeast in warm water and let work for 5 minutes. Whisk in milk mixture. Then add egg and flour. Mix well. Put in greased bowl, turning so greased side is on top. Cover loosely with plastic wrap. Chill dough until double in bulk, for about 1 to 2 hours. Divide dough into 2 parts. Roll out each piece to a 10" x 14" rectangle. Spread each rectangle with half of Orange Filling mixture, roll up and cut into 12 pieces. Place in 2 greased 9" x 13" pans. Cover and let rise in warm place until double in bulk. Bake at 350° for 15 to 20 minutes. Invert pans when done.

SALSA SAUSAGE POTATO STRATA

1 (32-ounce) pkg. frozen
shredded hashbrowns
1/4 cup vegetable oil
1 pkg. spicy Italian
turkey sausage, broken
up and browned
1 1/2 cups salsa
1/2 cup Ranch dressing

5 eggs, beaten
1 cup milk
1 cup shredded Monterey
Jack cheese
1 cup shredded cheddar
cheese
Sour cream and chopped
cilantro, for garnish

Thaw potatoes and squeeze out extra moisture, then stir in oil and put in bottom of sprayed 9" x 13" pan. Bake at 450° for about 45 minutes, stirring occasionally, until lightly browned. Top with browned sausage. Mix salsa and Ranch dressing, spread over potatoes and sausage. Mix eggs and milk and pour over casserole. Top with cheeses. Bake at 350° for 45 minutes or until cheese bubbles. Garnish with sour cream and chopped cilantro. Serve with extra salsa on the side. Note: I do the potatoes the night before.

SPINACH & SUN-DRIED TOMATO QUICHE

2 tablespoons butter or margarine, melted
1 small chopped onion
4 ounces sliced fresh mushrooms
1 (10-ounce) pkg. thawed & chopped spinach, squeezed dry

1/3 cup oil-packed, sun-dried tomatoes, drained & chopped
5 eggs
2 cups half and half cream
1 cup ricotta cheese
1 large unbaked pie shell
1/4 cup Parmesan cheese

Melt butter and sauté onion and mushrooms until translucent and tender. Meanwhile, squeeze thawed spinach dry, and chop again. Mix together with sauteed vegetables. Add tomatoes. Beat eggs and half and half and add to vegetable mixture. Mix in ricotta cheese. Pour into pie shell. Sprinkle with Parmesan cheese. Bake at 350° for 1 hour or until knife inserted in center comes out clean. Let rest for about 15 minutes before cutting and serving.

VANILLA FRENCH TOAST WITH FRESH STRAWBERRY RHUBARB SAUCE

2 pints strawberries, washed & sliced
2 - 3 stalks fresh rhubarb, washed & sliced
3/4 - 1 cup water
3/4 - 1 cup sugar

6 eggs
2 cups milk
1/4 cup sugar
2 tablespoons vanilla
2 teaspoons cinnamon
2 loaves French bread, cut into 18 thick slices

For Sauce: Wash strawberries and rhubarb and slice into a 2-quart saucepan. Add water and 3/4 - 1 cup sugar. Bring to a boil, then simmer until sauce is the right consistency and reduced. Adjust sweetness to taste. Sauce keeps in refrigerator for several days. For Vanilla French Toast: Mix eggs, milk, 1/4 cup sugar, vanilla and cinnamon. Dip bread slices in mixture and cook until golden brown on griddle that has been sprayed with Pam spray. Dust with powdered sugar and serve with Sauce on the side. Makes 6 servings.

Candlewycke Inn B&B

311 Aero Lane • Bigfork, MT 59911
406-837-6406 888-617-8805
406-837-9921 FAX
Web site: www.candlewyckeinn.com
E-mail: candle@digisys.net
Innkeeper: Megan Vandegrift

Six clean, spacious king and queen size country folk-art theme decorated suites and rooms, all with private baths. Quilts and antiques complement each room to provide a comfortable, quiet retreat to all travelers. Pillowtop beds ensure the best night's sleep you'll ever experience away from home. Bathrobes and beach towels are provided for each guest at the hot tub. King size rooms have TV's and refrigerators. Prices accommodate singles, couples, families and groups. Join me anytime of the year. Enjoy good food and a warm, friendly, relaxed atmosphere with so much to do, and only minutes away from unforgettable memories. Whether you fancy warm or cold weather activities, throughout all the seasons, we offer relaxation and recreation to fill your heart, mind, body and soul.

Rates: $$ - $$$$ Includes full breakfast. Children are welcome. No pets, please. Restricted smoking. We accept MasterCard and Visa.

Recipe From Candlewycke Inn B&B

GRAPE NUTS PARFAITS

Grape Nuts Granola:
1 cup Grape Nuts cereal
1 cup Wheaties cereal
2 cups old-fashioned oats
1 cup pecan halves
4 1/2 teaspoons
  wheat germ

1 teaspoon cinnamon
1/4 cup butter or
  margarine, melted
2 tablespoons maple
  syrup
2 tablespoons honey

Parfait Ingredients:
1 (22-ounce) carton
  Kozy Shack rice
  pudding
1 (20-ounce) can
  pineapple tidbits,
  drained

1 (15-ounce) can diced
  peaches with cinnamon,
  drained
1 (8-ounce) can
  mandarin oranges,
  drained

In a bowl combine cereals, oats, pecans, wheat germ and cinnamon. Combine butter, maple syrup and honey. Drizzle over the dry mixture. Pour into a greased 9" x 13" x 2" pan. Bake uncovered at 350° for 30 minutes, stirring every 10 minutes. Cool on a wire rack. Crumble into pieces. This can be done at anytime and stored in an airtight container. Mix together rice pudding and drained fruits. To assemble: In each parfait glass layer 4 tablespoons of Grape Nuts Granola mixture, then 4 tablespoons of fruit-pudding mixture. Repeat layers. Serve immediately, so granola stays crunchy. Use fresh fruits when in season, especially huckleberries or bananas, seedless grapes, strawberries, blueberries, etc. Makes 20 servings.

SHISH KEBOB OMELETS

1 (8-ounce) can pineapple chunks, drained (reserve juice)
Cut the following into medium pieces:
Mushrooms, to taste
Hillshire Farms Lite Polish Sausage or Turkey Kielbasa
Red peppers, onions, zucchini, yellow squash, grape or cherry tomatoes
1 firm banana

Marinade:
2 tablespoons Kraft Sun-Dried Tomato dressing
Reserved pineapple juice
3 tablespoons lite soy sauce

Additional Ingredients:
1 diced baby red potato, browned/person
1 scrambled egg/person

Prepare meat, vegetables and fruit. Prepare marinade. Marinate cut items in bowl or large baggie overnight. Prepare grill or set broiler on high and spray with Pam. Place 2 cut pieces of each veggie, fruit and meat on each wooden skewer. Brush any remaining marinade on top. Grill or broil until tender and brown, for about 3 to 5 minutes on each side. Meanwhile, brown 1 potato per person and scramble 1 egg per person. Pour scrambled egg over potatoes for individual servings. Place 1 skewer on top of each egg/potato serving. Add healthy grain toast and additional fruit for a light, healthy, colorful meal. Some guests like to make their own skewer for a fun breakfast experience. Quick and easy and always a hit!

Recipes From Candlewycke Inn B&B

COFFEE BANANA SMOOTHIE

2 small bananas,
  peeled, cut up
  and frozen
1 1/2 cups skim milk
1 (8-ounce) container
  lowfat coffee yogurt

1/4 teaspoon ground
  cinnamon
Dash of ground nutmeg
Fresh bananas and
  chocolate covered
  coffee beans/garnish

In a blender combine frozen bananas, milk, yogurt, cinnamon and nutmeg. Cover and blend until smooth. To serve, pour into glasses. Garnish with fresh bananas and chocolate covered coffee beans. Makes 2 (1 1/2-cup) servings.

VEGGIE PUFF

1 tablespoon olive
  oil
1/4 cup O'Brien
  hashbrowns, with
  onions & peppers
  already added
2 mushrooms, cut into
  medium pieces
10 fresh spinach leaves,
  washed

2 asparagus stalks, cut
  into medium pieces
  and/or 2 broccoli florets
1/3 cup grated pepper
  jack cheese
3 corn tortilla chips,
  broken into pieces
2 eggs
Milk, as directed below
Salsa, for garnish

Heat oil in a small saucepan. Brown hashbrowns and mushrooms. Lay spinach leaves on top of browned veggies. Add asparagus and broccoli pieces on top of spinach leaves. Sprinkle with grated cheese. Top with broken chips. Beat 2 eggs in a 2-cup measuring cup. Add enough milk to make 1 cup total liquid; beat again. Pour over all the ingredients in the pan. The egg mixture won't cover yet. It will puff up during cooking time. Turn the heat down low, cover with a lid and let slow cook for about 15 minutes until egg sets and cheese is melted. Cut in half and serve with salsa. Makes 2 servings. (Double ingredients and size of pan for 4 - cut into quarters to serve.)

Carolina Bed & Breakfast

309 North Ewing • Helena, MT 59601
406-495-8095   406-495-0051 FAX
Web site: www.carolinab-b.com
E-mail: carolina@mt.net
Innkeepers: Colleen Cox and Rene Requa

We invite you to share in the splendor of this magnificent turn-of-the-century home located in the heart of Helena's historic district. The original craftsmanship, from mahogany woodwork to extensive Tiffany glass, reflect the luxury of Helena's colorful past. *The Carolina* is ideally appointed for the vacationer and business traveler, with six exquisite bedrooms featuring private baths, private phone lines, air conditioning and cable TV. Across from the Original Governor's Mansion, *The Carolina* is a short walk from St. Helena's Cathedral and architecturally-rich downtown Helena. The spacious air-conditioned third floor includes two conference rooms, a library and complete business center available to all guests.

Rates: $$$ Includes full breakfast. Children are welcome.
Restricted smoking. Main floor room available. We accept
MasterCard, Visa and Am Ex.

LUS KRINGLE PASTRY

Topping Mixture:
1 cup water
1/2 cup butter
1 cup flour
3 eggs
1/2 teaspoon almond
  extract

Pastry Dough:
1 cup flour
1/2 cup soft butter
1 tablespoon water

Frosting:
1 1/2 tablespoons soft
  butter
2 tablespoons cream

1/2 teaspoon almond
  extract
Powdered sugar, to taste

Mix pastry dough ingredients together like pie crust. Put on cookie sheet and make two 15" x 3" strips by flattening with your fingers. For Topping: Heat water and butter to boiling. Remove from heat and add flour; stir until smooth. Beat in eggs, one at a time (do not pre-beat eggs). Add almond extract. Spread mixture on strips. Bake at 400° for 45 minutes. Stir together Frosting ingredients, adding enough powdered sugar to thicken. Frosting should be quite thin. Frost pastry.

SPINACH & EGGS CAROLINA

Butter, as needed
1 head spinach, rinsed
6 eggs

2 tablespoons feta
  cheese
Salt & pepper, to taste

Melt small amount of butter in frying pan. Rinse and drain spinach and place in frying pan with butter. Break eggs on top of spinach, then sprinkle with feta cheese. Add salt and pepper, to taste. Cover and cook until eggs are firm, but yolks are soft.

Carriage House Ranch Bed & Breakfast

771 Highway 191 North - P.O. Box 1249
Big Timber, MT 59011-1249
406-932-5339   877-932-5339
406-932-5863 FAX
Web site: www.carriagehouseranch.com
E-mail: chr@carriagehouseranch.com
Innkeepers: John Haller and Sally DeStefano

Your perfect private getaway in Montana awaits you at the *Carriage House Ranch Bed & Breakfast.* The inn, a renovated 1910 Dutch carriage house, exudes warmth and casual elegance in a serene ranch setting, located at the edge of a tranquil creek that overlooks the Crazy Mountains. Enjoy quiet privacy at the inn, or the excitement of the ranch's year-round equine events center schedule. Horse training, rider instruction, overnight stabling and kenneling are available. Custom-designed vacations to fit your dreams! Private parties, weddings, meetings, special dinners, events, competition and carriage ride reservations. Explore the area's wilderness, fly fish the nearby Yellowstone and Boulder Rivers or drop a line in Big Timber Creek which runs through *Carriage House Ranch.* Hike, observe nature and abundant wildlife, take a riding lesson and trail ride the ranch's 700 acres of natural scenic Montana beauty. Lewis & Clark Trail. Three bedrooms available.

Rates: $$$$ Includes full breakfast. Children over age 6 are welcome. Pets allowed. No smoking, please. We accept MasterCard and Visa.

FAT-FREE BANANA MUFFINS
IN FOOD PROCESSOR

2 bananas, pureed in
  food processor
1/2 cup applesauce
1 1/2 cups + 1/4 cup flour
3/4 cup sugar
2 eggs
1 teaspoon baking soda

1/4 cup milk
1 teaspoon vanilla
1 tablespoon white
  vinegar
1 teaspoon baking
  powder
Granola, for topping

Puree bananas in food processor. Add remaining ingredients. Blend only until just blended; do not overmix. Fill muffin cups and top with granola. Bake at 350° for 15 minutes or more, depending on altitude. Makes 6 servings.

FRESH ORANGE & CRANBERRY COMPOTE

1 1/2 cups fresh
  cranberries
1/3 cup sugar
1/4 cup water
Dash of cinnamon

4 juice oranges, peeled
  & sliced into rounds,
  seeded
1 tablespoon grated
  orange peel

Put cranberries in small skillet and sprinkle sugar over them. Add water and cook over low heat, stirring often. Cook until sugar has dissolved and cranberries have popped, for about 3 or 4 minutes. Remove skillet from heat and add cinnamon, orange slices and grated orange peel. Gently stir, spooning cranberry juice over slices until saturated. Serve warm or chilled. Excellent over warm scones, topped with whipped cream. Makes 2 cups.

Charley Montana Bed & Breakfast

103 North Douglas • Glendive, MT 59330
406-365-3207 (Phone & FAX)
888-395-3207
Web site: charley-montana.com
E-mail: charley@midrivers.com
Innkeepers: Jim and Katherine Lee

Eastern Montana's badlands are surprisingly beautiful, with opportunities for off-the-grid hiking, biking, canoeing and historic exploration. Glendive is a historic cattle town nestled in the rugged buttes where I-94 meets the untamed Yellowstone River. Glendive is a 9 1/2-hour drive from Minneapolis. Hit the parks: Makoshika (Montana's largest state park), 10 minutes; Yellowstone National Park, 5 hours; Glacier National Park, 10 hours; Theodore Roosevelt National Park, 1 1/2 hours. *Charley Montana Bed & Breakfast*, one of Montana's premier historic residences, was built by rancher Charles Krug in 1907. The 8,000 square foot, 25-room Krug Mansion is on the National Register. Guests enjoy seven comfortably decorated guest rooms, private baths and queen size beds, dining room, sitting room, parlor, library and gallery halls, brick-walled recreation room and more. Group rates available. Visit our web site.

Rates: $$$ Includes full breakfast. Children over age 3 are welcome. No pets or smoking, please. We accept MasterCard, Visa and Am Ex.

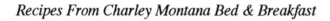

DONUT MUFFINS

2/3 cup vegetable oil
1 3/4 cups sugar, divided
2 eggs
3 cups flour
1/2 teaspoon salt
4 teaspoons baking
  powder

1/2 teaspoon nutmeg
1/2 teaspoon mace (the
  secret of the flavor!)
3 teaspoons cinnamon,
  divided
1 cup milk
3/4 cup melted butter

Preheat oven to 400°. Prepare 12 medium muffin cups with foil liners or spray with Baker's Joy. Cream together oil, 1 cup sugar and eggs. Sift together (or blend) flour, salt, baking powder, nutmeg, mace and 1/2 teaspoon cinnamon. Add dry ingredients to creamed mixture alternately with milk. Do not overmix or tunnels change the texture. Spoon into muffin pan and bake for approximately 20 minutes. Immediately remove from pan and remove liners. Roll muffins in melted butter, then into mixture of 3/4 cup sugar and 2 1/2 teaspoons cinnamon. Serve warm to happy people. Different, delicious and memorable! Send leftovers, if any, off with travelers.

POTATO PANCAKES

2 eggs
1/4 cup self-rising flour

3 cups raw potatoes,
  cubed

Heat griddle. Into blender container drop eggs and flour. (You may use 1/4 cup all-purpose flour, 1 teaspoon baking powder and 1/2 teaspoon salt for self-rising flour.) Peel and cube potatoes. Reserve 1/2 cup. Blend potatoes, eggs and flour until smooth, adding potatoes 1/2 cup at a time. Potatoes liquefy to create all the liquid in the pancakes. Blend reserved potatoes at the end so there is some potato texture. Cook on well-oiled griddle. Cook all the batter; potatoes start to turn color almost immediately. Cooked pancakes may be reheated as a snack. Makes 6 servings. Serve with rustic bacon, real maple syrup and apricot compote or warm chokecherry syrup.

Cottonwood Hill Farm Inn

2928 Whitefish Stage Road • Kalispell, MT 59901
406-756-6404   800-458-0893
406-756-8507 FAX
Web site: www.cottonwoodhillfarm.com
E-mail: CEI1@Digisys.net
Innkeepers: Charlie and Jennifer Horvath

Spacious and elegant 3-room *Inn* centrally located between Whitefish
and Kalispell in Montana's beautiful Flathead Valley. All of our large
rooms have private baths, in-room cable and antique four-poster beds.
We serve a full gourmet breakfast at whatever time you please,
afternoon drinks and hors d'oeuvres and fresh desserts in the evening.
We also offer a full meal plan option and picnics in the park. Short
drive to Glacier National Park, Flathead Lake and Big Mountain Ski
Resort. We offer golf packages and Flathead Lake boat tours.

*Rates: $$$ - $$$$ Includes full breakfast. Children over age 12 are
welcome. No pets, please. Restricted smoking. We accept
MasterCard, Visa and Am Ex.*

ARTICHOKE SOUP NICHOLAS

6 artichokes
1 cup chopped onion
4 cups chicken stock
2 cups water
1/2 cup whipping cream

1 tablespoon chopped chives
1 tablespoon chopped parsley
Salt & pepper, to taste

Cook artichokes in a large pot with onion, chicken stock and water. Simmer until artichokes are tender, for about 45 minutes. Remove artichokes, reserving broth. Separate leaves, remove and discard choke. Dice bottoms and set aside. Use spoon to scrape meat from the leaves, place in food processor. Add the reserved cooking liquid and onions, process until smooth. Return to pot, add remaining ingredients and artichoke bottoms. Heat through. Adjust seasonings. Serve immediately. Makes 4 servings.

SMOKED TROUT CAKES

1 pound smoked trout
1/4 cup finely chopped onion
1/4 cup fresh bread crumbs or cracker crumbs
1/8 cup minced red or yellow bell pepper
Salt & pepper, to taste

Dash of Worcestershire sauce
1 tablespoon chopped fresh parsley
1 tablespoon finely chopped fresh herbs
1 egg, slightly beaten
Butter, as needed for pan frying

Crumble trout and add remaining ingredients, except butter. Gently shape into six patties. Cover and refrigerate for one hour. Melt butter in a heavy skillet over medium heat. Cook patties until lightly golden on both sides. May be kept warm in a low oven. Serve with poached eggs and Hollandaise sauce for a nice variation on Eggs Benedict.

Cottonwood Inn Bed & Breakfast

13515 Cottonwood Canyon Road • Bozeman, MT 59718
406-763-5452   888-879-4667
406-763-5639 FAX
Web site: www.cottonwood-inn.com
E-mail: info@cottonwood-inn.com
Innkeepers: Joe and Debbie Velli

The Cottonwood Inn is a very personal place, where you are welcome to finish the half-solved puzzle on the antique table by the fire, or to play your favorite melody on the baby grand piano. The area is home to moose, elk, deer and other wildlife which can be viewed from your window or the wraparound covered porch. Named for nearby rivers, each of the 5 guest rooms has a private bath and incredible views. Enjoy the hot tub on moonlit evenings under Montana's Big Sky. Here in the winter, blue-shadowed ski trails are a few steps away. In summer, it's a short walk into the National Forest for hiking, biking and fishing. We're accessible by air or car, only 10 miles south of Bozeman and just 1 hour to Yellowstone National Park.

Rates: $$$ - $$$$ Includes full breakfast. Children over age 12 are welcome. No pets, please. Restricted smoking. We accept MasterCard, Visa and Am Ex.

❖ *Recipes From Cottonwood Inn Bed & Breakfast* ❖

APPLE-CRANBERRY BREAKFAST BAKE

4 cups skim milk
1/2 cup packed brown
  sugar
1/2 teaspoon salt
6 ounces golden raisins
2 cups uncooked old-
  fashioned oatmeal

3 medium Red Delicious
  apples, cored & sliced
1 cup fresh cranberries
1/4 cup brown sugar
1 cup chopped nuts
Nonfat sour cream, sugar
  & cinnamon, to taste

Preheat oven to 350°. In microwave-safe bowl add milk, 1/2 cup brown sugar and salt. Microwave until very hot, but not boiling. Add raisins, oatmeal, apples and cranberries coated with 1/4 cup brown sugar and nuts. Mix well. Put into stoneware serving/cooking bowl and bake for 30 minutes. Stir before putting into oven-proof bowls. Top with a "dollop" of nonfat sour cream, sweetened with sugar and cinnamon. Makes 8 - 12 servings.

ITALIAN FRITTATA WITH SAUSAGE SAUCE

Vegetable Sauce:
8 ounces country sausage
2 tablespoons butter
1 medium onion, sliced
1 clove garlic, minced
5 medium peppers (green,
  red or yellow), seeded
  & sliced lengthwise
4 cups diced Roma
  tomatoes
1/2 cup fresh basil,
  chopped
1 1/4 teaspoons salt

Frittata:
10 eggs
3/4 cup sour
  cream
3/4 teaspoon salt
1/4 teaspoon pepper
2 tablespoons fresh
  chopped basil
1/2 cup chopped green
  onion
2/3 cup grated Parmesan
  cheese

For Sauce: In a skillet cook sausage and let cool. Melt butter, sauté onion and garlic. Add peppers and cook for 5 minutes. Stir in tomatoes, basil and salt. Bring to a boil, then simmer until liquid is reduced by half. Add sausage; set aside. For Frittata: In mixing bowl whisk eggs, sour cream, salt and pepper. In 10" oven-proof skillet add basil and onion, sauté for 1 minute. Pour egg mixture into skillet, cover and cook over medium heat until eggs are set. Remove from heat, sprinkle with cheese. Broil until cheese melts. Serve with Sauce. Makes 8 - 10 servings.

Eagle Rock Hideaway Bed & Breakfast

P.O. Box 298 - 77 Hilltop Trail • Ennis, MT 59729
406-682-5715 (Phone & FAX)
Web site: www.eaglerockhideaway.com
E-mail: eglrock@3rivers.net
Innkeepers: Bill and Marcia Zankowski

The Last Best Place, Montana, and our inn is a "little bit of paradise up on a knoll." We have 3 guest rooms, 2 with queen beds and 1 with a king. Our beds are super comfortable with pillow top mattresses. We also offer a package deal, 2 rooms for the price of 1, if staying 2 nights or more, for parties of 3 or more. All rooms have private baths. Delicious food. Come and see us.

Rates: $ - $$$ Includes full breakfast. No children or pets, please. Restricted smoking. Handicapped accessible.

BAKED SAUSAGE PATTIES

3/4 cup soft bread crumbs
1 tablespoon chopped
  onion
1 egg

1/2 teaspoon salt
1/8 teaspoon pepper
6 ounces bulk pork
  sausage

Mix all ingredients well. Form into patties and place into a sprayed baking pan. Bake at 350° for 15 to 20 minutes until golden brown. Serve. Makes 4 sausage patties. Nice to have baking while preparing the rest of the breakfast.

FROZEN FRUIT CUPS

1 (15-ounce) can fruit
  cocktail, drained
1 (15-ounce) can
  pineapple tidbits,
  drained
1 small jar red
  maraschino cherries,
  drained & cut in halves

1 (3-ounce) pkg. cream
  cheese
1 (8-ounce) carton
  Cool Whip
1 teaspoon vanilla
1/4 teaspoon almond
  flavoring
Fresh fruit/mint garnish

Mix all drained fruit together in a bowl. Mix together cream cheese, Cool Whip, vanilla and almond flavoring well with a mixer. Stir together fruits and cream mixture. Pour into muffin tins lined with paper baking cups. Garnish each one with an additional cherry. Freeze. To serve, remove from freezer and let stand at room temperature for 10 to 15 minutes. Remove paper and place frozen fruit cup in a small serving dish. Garnish with fruit such as strawberries, peaches or whatever and a mint leaf. This is a nice starter for breakfast, especially in the summer.

Recipes From Eagle Rock Hideaway Bed & Breakfast

BUTTERMILK SYRUP

1/4 cup butter or
  margarine
1 tablespoon white
  corn syrup

1 cup sugar
3/4 cup buttermilk
1 teaspoon vanilla
  extract

Combine butter, corn syrup and sugar in a saucepan. Bring to a boil and boil and stir for 5 minutes. Stir in buttermilk and vanilla. Let stand for 5 minutes. Stir and serve with Oatmeal Pancakes (see recipe on page 51). This is a nice change from maple syrup. Makes about 1 1/2 cups syrup.

MAPLE STICKY BUNS

2 packages dry
  yeast
2 cups warm water
  (110° - 115°)
1/4 cup shortening
1/2 cup sugar
2 teaspoons salt
1 egg
6 - 6 1/2 cups flour

6 tablespoons soft
  margarine or butter
3/4 cup packed brown
  sugar
3/4 cup chopped walnuts
1 tablespoon ground
  cinnamon
1 1/2 cups maple syrup
Additional brown sugar

In mixing bowl dissolve yeast in water. Add shortening, sugar, salt, egg and enough flour to form a soft dough. Cover and refrigerate for 24 hours. Punch dough down. Turn out onto floured surface, knead 6 to 8 minutes until smooth and elastic, adding more flour if needed. Divide dough into thirds. Roll each portion into a 15" x 10" rectangle. On each rectangle spread 2 tablespoons butter, 1/4 cup brown sugar, 1/4 cup chopped walnuts and 1 teaspoon cinnamon. Divide maple syrup and pour into 3 (9") round baking pans. Sprinkle with brown sugar. Roll up each rectangle tightly, jellyroll style, starting with the short side. Slice each roll into 10 pieces; place over syrup. Cover and let rise until doubled, for about 30 minutes. Bake at 350° for 20 to 30 minutes or until golden brown. Cool for 5 minutes and then invert on a wire rack. Makes 2 1/2 dozen buns.

OATMEAL PANCAKES

1 cup whole wheat flour
1 cup old-fashioned oats
1/4 cup wheat germ
2 tablespoons flax seed
1/4 cup dry milk powder

1 tablespoon brown sugar
1 teaspoon baking soda
2 eggs
2 cups buttermilk
1/4 cup oil

Combine all dry ingredients in a bowl. Blend eggs, buttermilk and oil together and pour into the dry ingredients, mixing only until just blended. Pour out onto a hot griddle and bake until bubbles form on top. Flip and cook until golden brown. Makes 16 pancakes. Serve with Buttermilk Syrup (see recipe on page 50).

PEACH FRENCH TOAST

1 (29-ounce) can sliced
   peaches, drained
   (reserve syrup)
1 cup brown sugar
1/2 cup butter or
   margarine

2 tablespoons water
1 loaf French bread,
   sliced into 12 - 14 slices
5 eggs
1 tablespoon vanilla
1 1/2 cups milk

For Peach Syrup:
Reserved peach juice
1/4 cup brown sugar

1 1/2 tablespoons
cornstarch

Drain peaches and reserve syrup. Heat brown sugar and butter on medium-low heat until melted. Add water and cook until thick and foamy. Pour into a 9" x 13" baking dish. Cool for 10 minutes. Place peach slices in cooled caramel sauce. Cover with slices of bread placed close together. In blender add eggs, vanilla and milk, blend until well mixed. Pour over bread and refrigerate overnight. Bake at 350° for 40 minutes. Cover with foil if browning too quickly. Add brown sugar and cornstarch to reserved peach juice; cook until thick. Serve Toast with warm Peach Syrup and whipped cream on top. Sprinkle with cinnamon or chopped pecans. Makes 9 servings. Very good and easy to prepare. Nice to serve with sausage, juice, assorted rolls and muffins and a starter parfait.

Fox Hollow Bed & Breakfast
And Guest House

545 Mary Road • Bozeman, MT 59718
406-582-8440   800-431-5010
406-582-9752 FAX
Web site: bozeman-mt.com
E-mail: foxhollow@bozeman-mt.com
Innkeepers: Michael and Nancy Dawson

The wonder of Montana's Big Sky awaits you at *Fox Hollow Bed & Breakfast And Guest House*. Located in the Gallatin Valley near the friendly town of Bozeman, *Fox Hollow* combines luxury accommodations with panoramic mountain views and wide open spaces. Travelers find a relaxed atmosphere surrounded by the peace of a country setting. Five oversized guest rooms, each with a view of the Rockies, feature plush queen sized beds and private baths. Greet each morning with a delicious gourmet breakfast featuring such specialties as Eggs Benedict, baked omelets, homemade pastries and petite caramel rolls. In the evenings, settle down to a book or conversation in our comfortable living room, or join us by the fire in our family room. View the sunset, the stars or the shocking blue of the Big Sky from our wraparound deck, or indulge in a soothing soak in the hot tub. Come join Michael and Nancy and their friendly Montana hospitality.

Rates: $$$ - $$$$ Includes full breakfast. Children over age 12 are welcome. No pets, please. Restricted smoking. We accept MasterCard, Visa, Am Ex and Discover.

❖ *Recipes From Fox Hollow Bed & Breakfast And Guest House* ❖

BLUEBERRY FRENCH TOAST

1 loaf day-old white bread, crusts removed and cut into 1" cubes
1 (8-ounce) pkg. cream cheese, softened
2 tablespoons sugar

1/2 teaspoon maple flavoring
1 cup blueberries, fresh or frozen
4 whole eggs
1 1/2 cups milk
1/3 cup maple syrup

Sauce:
1 cup sugar
2 tablespoons cornstarch
1 cup water

1 cup blueberries, fresh or frozen
1 tablespoon butter

Remove crusts from bread and cut into 1" cubes, place half in a greased 9" x 13" x 2" baking dish. Combine cream cheese, sugar and maple flavoring. Drop random spoonfuls over bread layer. Top with 1 cup blueberries and remaining bread cubes. In large bowl beat eggs. Add milk and maple syrup; mix well. Pour over bread. Cover and refrigerate overnight. Remove from refrigerator 30 minutes before baking. Bake at 350° for 35 minutes. For Sauce: Combine sugar and cornstarch; add water. Bring to boil over medium heat; boil for three minutes, stirring constantly. Stir in 1 cup blueberries; reduce heat. Simmer for 8 to 10 minutes or until blueberries have burst. Stir in butter. Serve Sauce over French Toast. Makes 8 servings.

CRUSTLESS HAM QUICHE

1/2 pound fresh thinly sliced mushrooms
2 tablespoons butter
4 whole eggs
1 cup sour cream
1 cup small curd cottage cheese
1/2 cup Parmesan cheese

4 tablespoons flour
1 teaspoon onion powder
1/4 teaspoon salt
4 drops Tabasco sauce
2 cups jack cheese, shredded
1 cup ham, diced

Sauté mushrooms in butter until tender. Remove with slotted spoon and drain on paper towel. In food processor blend remaining ingredients (except ham and jack cheese). Pour mixture into large bowl. Add mushrooms, jack cheese and ham. Pour into 9" - 10" quiche pan and bake at 350° for 45 minutes. Makes 6 servings.

FANCY VEGETABLE & CHEESE ROULADE

1 cup milk
6 whole eggs
1/2 cup flour
2 tablespoons melted
  butter
1/2 teaspoon salt
1/2 teaspoon onion
  powder
1/4 teaspoon white pepper
Olive oil, to sauté

1/2 cup red bell peppers,
  chopped
1/2 cup yellow bell
  peppers, chopped
1/2 cup mushrooms,
  chopped
1/2 cup onions, chopped
1/2 cup fresh spinach
1 cup shredded cheddar
  cheese

Preheat oven to 350°. Line bottom and sides of 15" x 10" jellyroll pan with foil. Generously spray bottom and sides with nonstick cooking spray. Combine milk, eggs, flour, butter and seasonings in medium bowl. Beat with mixer until well blended. Pour into prepared pan. Bake for 10 minutes. Meanwhile sauté peppers, mushrooms and onions in small amount of olive oil until softened and tender. Add spinach & sauté for one minute or until just softened. When eggs are beginning to set, sprinkle with vegetables. Continue baking for 8 to 10 minutes longer or until eggs are set, but not dry. Remove from oven and immediately sprinkle with cheese. Beginning with short end of omelet, carefully roll up, using foil to gently lift it from pan. Transfer omelet to platter & cut into 1 1/4" slices. Makes 4 servings.

FRESH BERRIES & CREME

2 tablespoons sugar
2 teaspoons cornstarch
1 cup skim milk
1 whole beaten egg
2 tablespoons light
  sour cream

1/2 teaspoon vanilla
<u>Serve over:</u>
3 cups fresh berries:
  raspberries, black-
  berries, blueberries,
  strawberries, etc.

Combine sugar and cornstarch in small saucepan. Add milk and beaten egg. Cook and stir with wooden spoon just until mixture begins to bubble. (Do not overcook.) Immediately pour custard out of saucepan into a small bowl; let cool for 5 minutes. Whisk sour cream into mixture; add vanilla. Cover and thoroughly chill custard for up to 24 hours. Serve over fresh berries. Makes 8 servings.

FRUIT & GRANOLA PARFAITS

1/2 cup vanilla yogurt,
  nonfat or light
1/4 cup light or nonfat
  cream cheese
1 tablespoon honey
1/4 teaspoon cinnamon
2 whole kiwi fruits,
  peeled, halved & sliced

1 whole banana, sliced
1 whole orange, peeled,
  cut into fourths & sliced
1 1/2 cups frozen
  raspberries, thawed
  & drained
1 cup lowfat granola
  cereal

Combine yogurt, cream cheese, honey and cinnamon; beat with electric mixer on medium speed until combined. Chill. To assemble: Stir together fruit (you should have about 3 cups). Divide 1/3 of fruit mixture among 4 wine goblets. Spoon about 2 tablespoons each of cream cheese mixture and granola atop fruit. Repeat. Top with remaining fruit and serve immediately. Makes 4 servings. Fruit options: Strawberries, banana, kiwi, oranges, grapes, pears, blueberries. I use all fresh fruits - whatever is in season. Enjoy!

FUDGE BROWNIES

1 1/3 cups flour
2 cups sugar
3/4 cup cocoa
1 teaspoon baking
  powder
1/2 teaspoon salt

1/2 cup chopped nuts
2/3 cup cooking oil
4 whole eggs,
  slightly beaten
2 teaspoons vanilla
  extract

Combine flour, sugar, cocoa, baking powder, salt and nuts. Set aside. Combine oil, eggs and vanilla; add to dry ingredients. Do not overmix. Spread in a 9" x 13" x 2" baking pan. Bake at 350° for 20 to 25 minutes until toothpick inserted in center comes out clean. Makes about 2 dozen brownies.

Recipes From Fox Hollow Bed & Breakfast and Guest House

FOX HOLLOW
ZIPPY ARTICHOKE OVEN OMELET

3/4 cup salsa or
picante sauce
1 (14-ounce) can
artichoke hearts,
chopped
1/4 cup Parmesan
cheese, grated

1 cup jack cheese or
mozzarella cheese,
shredded
1 cup cheddar cheese,
shredded
6 whole eggs
1 cup sour cream

Grease a 10" quiche dish. Spread salsa in bottom. Distribute artichokes evenly over sauce. Sprinkle with Parmesan, jack and cheddar cheeses. In food processor blend eggs until smooth, add sour cream and blend. Pour into dish. Bake uncovered, at 350° for 45 minutes to 1 hour, until set. Cut into wedges and serve with sour cream, tomato wedges and parsley. Makes 6 servings.

JIFFY CINNAMON ROLLS

4 - 5 cups flour, divided
1 (9-ounce) package
1-layer white cake mix
2 packets quick-rise
active dry yeast
1 teaspoon salt

2 cups warm water
(120° - 130°)
2 tablespoons butter
1/2 cup sugar
1 tablespoon
cinnamon

In large mixing bowl combine 3 cups flour, cake mix, yeast, salt and warm water; mix until smooth. Add enough remaining flour to form a soft dough. Turn out onto lightly floured surface; knead until smooth, for about 6 to 8 minutes. Roll dough into a 9" x 18" rectangle. Spread with butter and sprinkle with sugar and cinnamon. Roll up jellyroll style, starting with long end. Slice roll into 1" circles, place on greased cookie sheet. Cover and let rise in warm place until doubled, for about 15 minutes. Bake at 350° for 15 to 18 minutes. Frost, if desired. Note: I butter the tops the last 10 minutes of baking to help them brown. Makes 18 rolls.

Recipe From Fox Hollow Bed & Breakfast and Guest House

LEMON POPPY SEED SANDWICHES
WITH LEMON CREAM FILLING

6 tablespoons butter
6 tablespoons shortening
1 cup sugar
2 eggs
3/4 cup milk
4 tablespoons lemon
 juice
3 cups all-purpose flour
2 teaspoons baking
 powder

1 teaspoon salt
1/4 cup poppy seeds

Lemon Cream Filling:
1 cup mascarpone cheese
1/2 cup sugar
1/4 cup lemon juice
1/2 cup heavy cream
1/4 cup confectioners
 sugar

Preheat oven to 350°. Grease a 9" x 5" loaf pan. Cream together butter, shortening and 1 cup sugar. Beat together eggs, milk and 4 tablespoons lemon juice. Mix together flour, baking powder and salt. Alternately add the wet ingredients and the dry to the butter-sugar mixture. Stir in poppy seeds. Spread batter in prepared loaf pan. Bake for 55 minutes or until toothpick comes out clean. Allow to cool thoroughly. Cut into approximately 18 (1/2") thick slices. For Filling: In medium bowl or with electric mixer, whisk together mascarpone and 1/2 cup sugar until smooth. Stir in 1/4 cup lemon juice. Whip cream to soft peaks and fold into the mascarpone mixture. Spread a slice of poppy seed loaf with cream filling and top with another slice, making a small sandwich. Repeat until all slices are used. Cut sandwiches in half, dust with confectioners sugar and serve. Bread may be frozen (unfilled) for up to 1 month and defrosted before serving. Filling may be made up to 24 hours in advance. Sandwiches may be assembled up to 24 hours ahead and refrigerated until serving.

Recipe From Fox Hollow Bed & Breakfast and Guest House

MACADAMIA-FUDGE CAKE

1 cup all-purpose flour
3/4 cup sugar
3/4 cup sour cream
1/2 cup butter, softened
1/4 cup cocoa
1 1/2 teaspoons instant coffee, powder or granules

1/2 teaspoon baking soda
1/2 teaspoon baking powder
1/2 teaspoon vanilla extract
1/4 teaspoon salt
1 whole egg

<u>Fudge-Nut Topping</u>:
1 cup whipping cream
1/2 cup sugar
2 tablespoons butter
1 tablespoon corn syrup

4 ounces semi-sweet chocolate
1 teaspoon vanilla extract
1 (7-ounce) jar macadamia nuts

Make cake about 3 hours before serving or a day ahead. Preheat oven to 350°. Grease 9" round cake pan; line bottom with wax paper and grease paper. In large bowl with mixer on low speed, beat all cake ingredients until blended, occasionally scraping bowl. Pour batter into pan. Bake for 30 to 35 minutes or until toothpick inserted in center comes out clean. Cool on wire rack for 10 minutes. Remove cake from pan; discard wax paper and cool cake completely. When cake is cool, prepare Topping. In 2-quart saucepan over medium-high heat, heat whipping cream, sugar, butter, corn syrup and chocolate to boiling, stirring constantly. Reduce heat to medium; cook for 5 minutes, stirring constantly. Remove saucepan from heat, stir in vanilla. Cool chocolate for about 10 minutes. Stir in nuts. Place cooled cake on plate, then quickly pour Topping evenly over cake, allowing some to run down the side. Refrigerate cake until topping is firm, for about 1 hour. For the holidays, garnish cake with pine boughs and Christmas balls. Holly is nice also. I also make this as a 2-layer cake by making 2 cakes and 1 1/2 recipes of the Topping.

❖ *Recipe From Fox Hollow Bed & Breakfast and Guest House*

CHOCOLATE COVERED RAISIN OATMEAL COOKIES

1/3 cup flaked coconut
1 1/2 cups flour
1/4 teaspoon baking powder
1 teaspoon salt
1 cup unsalted butter, softened
6 tablespoons solid vegetable shortening
1 1/4 cups brown sugar, firmly packed

1 cup granulated sugar
2 whole large eggs
1 tablespoon vanilla
2 1/2 cups quick-cooking oatmeal (not instant)
30 ounces semi-sweet, chocolate-covered raisins
1 1/4 cups coarsely chopped walnuts

Preheat oven to 325°. Line several cookie sheets with parchment paper. Place coconut in work bowl of food processor fitted with steel blade. Cover and process until finely chopped, for about 5 to 6 pulses; set aside. In bowl whisk together flour, baking powder and salt. In 4 1/2-quart bowl of heavy duty mixer, using the paddle attachment, cream butter and shortening on low speed for 4 minutes. Add brown sugar and continue beating at moderate speed for 1 minute. Add granulated sugar and beat for 1 minute longer. Beat in eggs, one at a time. Add vanilla and coconut, beat for 10 seconds. On low speed, add whisked flour mixture, beat just until particles of flour are absorbed. Stir in oatmeal, raisins and nuts. Drop scant 1/4 cup size mounds of dough onto cookie sheets, about 2" to 3" apart. Bake cookies for 14 to 16 minutes, or until just set and light golden brown around edges. Cool on sheets for 3 to 4 minutes, then remove to cooling rack, using a wide metal spatula. Makes about 36 cookies.

Recipe From Fox Hollow Bed & Breakfast And Guest House

PETITE PASTRIES

Filling:
1/4 cup brown sugar
3 tablespoons butter,
 softened
2 tablespoons flour
1 tablespoon cinnamon
1/3 cup pecans, finely
 chopped

1 (16-ounce) loaf frozen
 bread dough, thawed

Icing:
3 tablespoons butter
1 1/2 cups powdered
 sugar
3 tablespoons maple
 syrup
1 - 2 teaspoons milk

1 tablespoon milk, to
 brush sides of rolls

For Filling: Stir first four ingredients together and set aside. On lightly floured surface roll thawed dough to a 12" x 10" rectangle. Spread Filling on top, leaving 1/4" plain border. Sprinkle with nuts. Cut rectangle in half lengthwise (2 - 12" x 5" rectangles). Roll each rectangle jellyroll style starting from long side. Moisten edges and seal. Cut each log crosswise into 16 pieces. Arrange pieces 1" apart on greased baking sheet. Let raise, covered, in a warm place until nearly double, for about 25 minutes. Brush sides of rolls with milk. Bake at 350° for 10 to 15 minutes. Cool and frost. For Icing: In saucepan heat 3 tablespoons butter over medium-low heat for 7 to 10 minutes or until butter is light brown. Remove from heat and stir in powdered sugar and maple syrup. Stir in just enough milk to make icing of drizzling consistency. Makes 10 servings.

PUMPKIN MOUSSE WITH SUGARED PECANS

1/2 cup pecans, chopped
1 tablespoon light
brown sugar
1 (16-ounce) can solid-
pack pumpkin, not
pumpkin pie mix
1 (3-ounce) box instant
vanilla pudding &
pie filling

1 cup milk
1 teaspoon vanilla
3/4 teaspoon cinnamon
1/2 teaspoon ginger
1/2 teaspoon allspice
1/3 cup brown sugar,
firmly packed
2 cups whipping cream,
whipped

Make about 1 1/4 hours before serving or early in day. Prepare sugared pecans: Cook pecans in 2-quart saucepan over medium-high heat until lightly browned, stirring occasionally. Stir in 1 tablespoon brown sugar until sugar melts and evenly coats pecans. Set aside to cool. In large bowl with wire whisk mix pumpkin, pudding mix, milk, vanilla, spices and 1/3 cup brown sugar until blended. Whip cream until stiff peaks form. Refrigerate one cup whipped cream for garnish. Fold remaining whipped cream into pumpkin mixture. Spoon mousse into 8 (10-ounce) goblets; cover and refrigerate until ready to serve. To serve, spoon reserved whipped cream onto mousse; sprinkle with pecans. Makes 8 servings.

WHITE-CHOCOLATE CAFÉ AU LAIT

12 ounces melted white
chocolate
3 cups whole milk,
scalded
6 tablespoons instant
espresso powder

3 teaspoons sugar or
cinnamon
1 ounce white chocolate,
shaved
6 whole cinnamon
sticks

Pour 2 ounces melted chocolate per cup into 6 (12-ounce) mugs or coffee cups. Add scalded milk and espresso. Top each serving with sugar or cinnamon, chocolate shavings and cinnamon sticks. Serve immediately. Makes 6 servings.

Johnstad's Bed & Breakfast and Log Cabin

P.O. Box 981 - 03 Paradise Lane • Emigrant, MT 59027
406-333-9003 (Phone & FAX)   800-340-4993
Web site: www.wtp.net/go/johnstad
E-mail: rjohnstad@aol.com
Innkeepers: Ron and Mary Ellen Johnstad

Johnstad's Bed & Breakfast and Log Cabin offers classic Montana hospitality in the heart of Paradise Valley. Our three spacious guest rooms all have private baths (one with a jetted tub) and spectacular views of the Absoraka Mountains and the Yellowstone River Valley. Each room is uniquely decorated to create a warm atmosphere. Our breakfasts are hearty, spiced with lively conversation and enjoyed either on the deck or in our dining room while viewing bald eagles, deer and other wildlife. Our *Log Cabin*, with panoramic views of Paradise Valley, is fully furnished with kitchen, dining area, living room, three bedrooms, two baths and laundry facilities. Blue ribbon fly fishing awaits you at our site - ask Ron, an avid fly fisherman, how to tie a fly. We offer connections for horseback riding, floating the Yellowstone River, hiking, soaking in hot springs and gourmet dining. And we are just 36 miles from the north entrance of Yellowstone National Park.

Rates: $$$ - $$$$ Includes full breakfast in B&B. Children are welcome in the Log Cabin. No pets or smoking, please. We accept MasterCard, Visa and Discover.

POPOVERS FILLED WITH SCRAMBLED EGGS

1 cup flour
1 cup cold water
2 eggs
1/2 teaspoon salt
6 eggs
6 tablespoons whipping
  cream
1 teaspoon chopped
  basil

Salt & pepper, to taste
Diced smoked turkey,
  to taste
2 ounces cream cheese
1/2 cup grated cheddar
  cheese
1/2 tablespoon butter
Parsley & grated cheese,
  for garnish

Blend flour, water, eggs and salt in a Cuisinart and pour into 4 greased ramekins. Place in cold oven and bake at 450° for 30 minutes. Scramble eggs, whipping cream, basil, seasonings, turkey, cream cheese and 1/2 cup grated cheese in butter. When eggs are set, slice the top off of the popovers & fill with scrambled eggs. Garnish with parsley and grated cheese. When serving tie a checkered bandana around the ramekin to protect hands from the heat. Makes 4 large servings.

RASPBERRY SMOOTHIE

1 cup raspberry yogurt
1 cup vanilla yogurt
2 cups orange juice

1 banana
1 cup raspberries
Fresh mint, for garnish

Use ripe fruit - the riper the fruit, the sweeter the smoothie. Process ingredients in a blender until smooth. Serve in goblets and garnish with a sprig of fresh mint. A refreshing way to start the morning, or renew energy after a hike in the mountains. Makes 6 - 8 servings.

Kootenai River Bed-N-Breakfast

1500 Forest Drive • Troy, MT 59935
406-295-1501 (Phone & FAX)
E-mail: rodding@libby.org
Innkeepers: Marsha Armstrong and Fred Charlton

We are nestled in the Cabinet Mountains, on the bank of the spectacular Kootenai River, 4 miles west of Troy, just off Highway 2. Enjoy breathtaking views, blue ribbon fly fishing and endless outdoor activities. Arrangements or support available for all activities. Stay with us and experience the last best place in Northwest Montana. We have 3 rooms, 2 with river view, all with private bath. Also a common room with fireplace and entertainment center for all to enjoy. Rooms: 1 king size log bed with river view, 1 queen size log bed with river view, 2 twin log beds in deluxe room. We have decorated all rooms in a fly-fishing theme for your enjoyment. If you are looking for a unique, peaceful and serene setting for your stay, this is the only place to be in Northwest Montana.

Rates: $$ - $$$$ Includes full breakfast. Children over age 10 are welcome. Small pets allowed. Restricted smoking. Handicapped accessible. We accept MasterCard and Visa.

FRUIT PIZZA

1 roll refrigerated sugar cookie dough (Pillsbury or any brand)
1 (8-ounce) pkg. cream cheese, softened
1/4 - 1/2 cup powdered sugar

1 teaspoon vanilla

Various fresh fruit: Bananas, peaches, kiwi, grapes, strawberries, any type of berries, sliced as desired

Pat cookie dough (you can use a small batch of homemade cookie dough) on ungreased baking sheet or baking stone in a circle the size of a pie plate. Bake at 350° for about 15 minutes or until evenly light brown. Cool. Whip cream cheese, powdered sugar and vanilla together. Spread on cooled crust. Arrange fruit slices on cream cheese layer, layered in circles around the crust. Slice as you would a pizza and serve. Can be refrigerated ahead of time, but bananas and kiwi need to be dipped in lemon juice to prevent them from turning brown. Makes 8 servings.

HASH BROWN QUICHE

1 (24-ounce) bag frozen uncooked shredded hashbrowns, thawed
5 tablespoons unsalted butter, melted
2 large eggs, beaten
1/2 cup half and half cream

1/2 teaspoon seasoned salt
1 cup jalapeno jack cheese, shredded
1 cup Swiss cheese, shredded
1 cup diced ham
Fresh parsley, for garnish

Preheat oven to 425°. Press hashbrowns into quiche pan. Blot with paper towel to remove all moisture. Brush with melted butter. Bake for 25 minutes. Remove from oven. Reduce oven temperature to 350°. Combine eggs, half and half and seasoned salt. Place cheeses and ham in hashbrown shell. Pour egg mixture over top. Bake for 40 to 50 minutes. Garnish with parsley. Makes 6 - 8 servings.

LEMON DUTCH BABY

3 egg whites
1 cup skim milk
1 cup all-purpose flour
2 teaspoons grated
  lemon rind
1/2 teaspoon poppy seeds

Cooking spray
1 tablespoon reduced-
  calorie margarine or
  butter
Powdered sugar
Maple syrup (opt.)

Place egg whites in container of blender and process on high for 1 minute. With blender on high, gradually add milk in slow, steady stream through opening in cover. Gradually add flour, 1 heaping spoonful at a time, process for 30 additional seconds. Add lemon rind and poppy seeds, process for 5 seconds. Coat a 10" cast iron skillet with cooking spray. Add margarine/butter to skillet and place in 425° oven for 5 minutes or until melted. Pour batter into hot skillet and bake for 20 minutes or until puffy and browned. Transfer pancake to a serving platter and sift powdered sugar over it. Serve immediately with maple syrup, if desired. Makes 4 servings.

SPINACH AND FETA PIE

1 (10-ounce) pkg. frozen
  chopped spinach,
  thawed & squeezed dry
1/2 cup crumbled feta
  cheese
4 medium green onions,
  sliced (1/4 cup)

1/2 cup Bisquick or
  other baking mix
3/4 cup milk
3 eggs
1/4 teaspoon salt
1/8 teaspoon pepper

Heat oven to 400°. Grease a 9" x 1 1/4" pie plate. Mix spinach, cheese and onions in pie plate. Stir remaining ingredients until blended and pour into pie plate. Bake for 30 to 35 minutes or until knife inserted in center comes out clean. Let stand for 5 minutes before serving. Makes 6 - 8 servings.

STICKY BUNS

20 frozen white
  dinner rolls
1/2 cup butter, melted
1/2 cup brown sugar

1 box cook & serve
  butterscotch pudding
Chopped pecans, to
  taste

Let rolls thaw for about 10 minutes. Cut a 1/2" slit into rolls. Spray
bundt pan with Pam spray. Put rolls into pan. Melt butter and pour
over rolls. In a bowl mix brown sugar, dry pudding mix and nuts.
Sprinkle over rolls. Cover with towel and let stand overnight. Bake
the next morning at 350° for 30 minutes. Turn onto plate and serve.

SWEDISH APPLE CAKE

2 cups sugar
1/2 cup shortening
2 eggs
2 cups flour
Pinch of salt
1 teaspoon cinnamon

1 teaspoon nutmeg
1 teaspoon baking soda
1 teaspoon baking powder
1 teaspoon vanilla
4 cups peeled, chopped
  apples

Preheat oven to 325°. Cream sugar and shortening; add eggs. Add
remaining ingredients. Add apples last. Bake in greased bundt pan,
greased 9" x 13" x 2" pan or greased large cupcake size (mini-bundt
pan). Bake for 35 minutes to 1 hour, depending on size of pan.
Bundt pan will be moist, 9" x 13" x 2" pan will be crunchy on top -
great for a breakfast group, mini-bundt is moist with crunchy top.
Freezes well. Makes 6 - 8 servings.

La Villa Montana

P.O. Box 1468 • Whitefish, MT 59937
406-862-8933   877-360-1413
Web site: www.lavilla.com
E-mail: TDKivela@Hotmail.com
Innkeepers: Diane and Tom Kivela

A country Scandinavian chalet set on 10 acres of beautifully timbered and landscaped meadowlands that are enjoyed by the surrounding wildlife; The *La Villa Montana* offers the most in Bed and Breakfast charm. *La Villa* is conveniently located on Montana Highway 40, just 2 1/2 miles east of junction 93 and 40 or 1 1/2 miles west of junction 2 and 40 in the beautiful Flathead Valley. The dining room and kitchen are centered around a classic brick fireplace. Enjoy a "stuffed-to-the-gills" home-cooked breakfast with all the trimmings. Languish in a soak in the outdoor hot tub. View the spectacular mountains from the expansive redwood deck. Take a leisurely stroll on the groomed trails through the wooded acreage. *La Villa's* four guest rooms provide everything from elegant styling to rustic charm; each affords a private bath. No matter which room you visit, each offers privacy, comfort and tranquility necessary to make your stay enjoyable.

Rates: $$$ - $$$$ Includes full breakfast. Children are welcome.
No pets or smoking, please. We accept MasterCard and Visa.

Recipes From La Villa Montana

BECKY'S DOUBLE FUDGE BARS

Filling:

1 (6-ounce) pkg. semi-sweet chocolate chips

1/2 cup butter

1 (14-ounce) can sweetened condensed milk

Crust:

1 cup butter, softened

1 cup sugar

1 cup packed brown sugar

2 eggs

1 1/2 cups flour

1/2 cup chocolate Malt-O-Meal, uncooked

1 teaspoon baking soda

3 cups rolled oats, uncooked

Preheat oven to 350°. For Filling: Melt chocolate chips and 1/2 cup butter over low heat (I use the microwave). Stir in sweetened condensed milk. Set aside. For Crust: Cream 1 cup softened butter and sugars; mix in eggs. Stir in dry ingredients. Reserve 1 1/2 cups of this mixture; press remaining mixture into greased 9" x 13" baking pan. Spread with chocolate filling. Crumble reserved mixture evenly over chocolate. Bake for 25 to 30 minutes or until center is soft, but crust and edges are firm. Cool and cut into bars. Makes 12 servings.

BLUEBERRY MUFFINS

1 cup margarine, at room temperature

2 cups sugar

4 eggs, slightly beaten

2 teaspoons vanilla

1/2 teaspoon salt

4 teaspoons baking powder

4 cups flour

1 cup milk

1 (16-ounce) pkg. frozen blueberries, not thawed

Topping:

2 tablespoons sugar

1/2 teaspoon nutmeg

Cream margarine and sugar. Add eggs and vanilla; mix thoroughly. Mix in salt, baking powder, flour and milk. Add blueberries and blend, stirring by hand. Spoon into 8 to 10 large Texas-size muffin tins until 2/3 full. Sprinkle with sugar-nutmeg topping mixture. Bake at 350° for 25 to 30 minutes.

FINNISH OVEN PANCAKES
Kropsu
(Pronounced krup'soo with a rolled "R")

3 eggs	1/2 cup sugar
2 cups milk	2 tablespoons oil
1 1/4 cups flour	1 teaspoon salt

Beat the eggs in a bowl until fluffy. Add milk, flour, sugar, oil and salt, beating continuously. The mixture should have the consistency of thick cream. Pour into a greased 9" x 13" pan. (Use a heavier type pan or glass pan.) The batter should be no more than one-half the depth of the pan. Bake in a very hot oven, at 400° for about 25 to 30 minutes or until lightly brown. It is best served immediately after baking. Serve with your favorite jam, syrup or honey. It also makes an excellent base for fresh berries in season. Use it as you would shortcake or add apples and spices on top. Makes 6 large servings.

GLACIER BREAKFAST BAKE

2 cups fully-cooked diced ham	1 tablespoon instant minced onion
1 (12-ounce) pkg. frozen hashbrown potatoes	2 cups shredded cheddar cheese, divided
1/2 cup fresh mushrooms	3 cups milk
1 cup chopped green bell peppers	1 cup Original Bisquick
	1/2 teaspoon salt
	4 eggs

Grease a 9" x 13" pan. Mix ham, potatoes, mushrooms, green pepper, onion and 1 cup cheese. Spread in pan. Stir milk, Bisquick, salt and eggs together until blended. Pour over potato mixture. Sprinkle with remaining 1 cup cheese. Cover and refrigerate for at least 4 hours, but no longer than 24 hours. Preheat oven to 375°. Bake uncovered for 30 to 35 minutes. Let stand for 10 minutes before serving. Makes 10 - 12 servings.

Recipes From La Villa Montana

GRANDMA'S APPLE CRISP

6 - 8 slightly tart apples
1/2 cup sugar
1 cup packed brown sugar
1 cup flour

1/2 cup butter, melted
1 cup rolled oats,
  uncooked
1/2 teaspoon cinnamon

Peel, core and slice apples into a 9" x 13" greased pan. Sprinkle 1/2 cup sugar on apple slices. Mix brown sugar, flour, melted butter, oats and cinnamon and crumble on top of apples. Bake at 350° for 45 minutes. Makes 10 - 12 servings.

JODY'S POPPY SEED BREAD

3 cups flour
2 1/4 cups sugar
1 1/2 tablespoons
  poppy seeds
1 1/2 teaspoons baking
  powder
1 1/2 teaspoons salt
3 eggs, lightly beaten

1 1/2 cups milk
1 cup vegetable oil
1 1/2 teaspoons vanilla
  extract
1 1/2 teaspoons almond
  extract
1 1/2 teaspoons butter
  extract

Glaze:
3/4 cup sugar
1/4 cup orange juice
1/2 teaspoon vanilla
  extract

1/2 teaspoon almond
  extract
1/2 teaspoon butter
  extract

For Bread: Combine first five ingredients. Add eggs, milk, oil and extracts. Pour into 2 greased and floured loaf pans. Bake at 350° for 60 to 65 minutes. Cool completely in pans. In a saucepan, bring all glaze ingredients to a boil. Pour over bread in pans. Cool for 5 minutes. Remove from pans.

The Montana Hotel
Historic Country Railroad Inn

P.O. Box 423 - 702 Railroad • Alberton, MT 59820
406-722-4990   888-271-9317
Web site: www.BedandBreakfast.com/alberton
E-mail: montanahotel@blackfoot.net
Innkeeper: Rebecca Hazlitt and Steve Young

Located at the "Gateway to the Alberton Gorge," Montana's best whitewater! Enjoy fishing, hunting, biking and hiking while "ruffing it" in authentic early 1900's atmosphere. Our ten eclectic rooms have private baths, TV and phones. Terrific breakfasts in our cheerful dining room or sunny courtyard are often accompanied by live harp music. Convenient for travelers - we are just off I-90, 30 miles west of Missoula. Great for group gatherings, especially folks who like to sing and play music!

Rates: $ - $$ Includes full breakfast. Children are welcome. Small, mature pets allowed for $5. No smoking, please. Handicapped accessible. We accept MasterCard and Visa.

SPICED POACHED PEARS

2 cups dry sherry or dry red wine	1 cinnamon stick, broken
1 cup cold water	6 whole cloves
1 tablespoon sugar	6 - 8 medium-sized, firm,
1 tablespoon lemon juice	ripe pears, cored & peeled, with stems on

Mix all ingredients except pears together in a crockpot. Turn on high for 1 hour. Then add pears and turn down to low setting. Baste pears with the liquid frequently as they cook on low for about 4 hours. Cool, and then refrigerate for at least 2 hours, up to 24 hours, basting occasionally. To serve: Place pears upright in a champagne-type goblet. Top with a generous dollop of Vanilla Sauce (see recipe below). Serves as many as there are pears.

VANILLA SAUCE FOR PEARS

2 cups milk, scalded	1/2 cup sugar
4 egg yolks, lightly beaten	1/8 teaspoon salt
	1 teaspoon vanilla

Scald milk in top of a double boiler over moderate heat. Whisk a little of the hot milk into the egg yolks, then stir the mixture back into the pan, and set over simmering water. Add sugar and salt. Stir constantly until the mixture begins to thicken, for about 3 minutes. Do not allow to boil or the sauce may curdle. Remove from the heat and stir in vanilla. Serve either chilled or warm over the cold pears (see recipe above).

Mountain Meadows Guest Ranch

7055 Beaver Creek Road • Big Sky, MT 59716
406-995-4997 888-644-6647
406-995-2097 FAX
Web site: www.mountainmeadowsranch.com
E-mail: mmgr@mcn.net
Innkeepers: The Severns

Accommodating up to 28 guests, *Mountain Meadows Guest Ranch's* goal is to make each guest's stay as intimate, exciting and memorable as possible. The Severn Family wants to share our love of the beautiful state of Montana and its treasures with you. Located 45 miles south of Bozeman and 18 miles north of Yellowstone National Park, this exclusive guest lodge is nestled among hundreds of acres of rolling meadows, lush forests, small ponds and bubbling streams. Surrounded by spectacular Lone Mountain, the Madison Mountain Range, the Spanish Peaks and the Gallatin Range, we offer breathtaking views from every angle. In summer, enjoy hiking, biking, a fly-fishing clinic, horseback riding, white-water rafting, golf, tennis, swimming and hayride/BBQ's. Winter features downhill and cross-country skiing, snowshoeing, sledding, tobogganing and sleigh rides. Guests use 2 log cabins and our 10,000 square foot log lodge with 7 guest rooms, dining room, sauna, jacuzzi, Thirsty Moose bar, rock fireplace and living area.

Rates: $$$$ Includes full breakfast. Children are welcome. No pets or smoking, please. Handicapped accessible. We accept MasterCard, Visa, Am Ex and Discover.

BEEFY BREAKFAST CASSEROLE

1 pound sliced bacon,
  diced & cooked
2 (4 1/2-ounce) pkgs.
  sliced dried beef (or
  any thinly sliced beef)
1 (4-ounce) can sliced
  mushrooms, drained
1/2 cup flour
1/8 teaspoon pepper
4 cups milk
16 eggs
1 cup evaporated milk
1/4 teaspoon salt
1/4 cup butter, melted

Cook bacon until crisp and drain. Save 1/4 cup of bacon drippings. Add beef, mushrooms, flour and pepper to the drippings and cook until thoroughly combined. Gradually add 4 cups milk and stir until thickened. Add cooked bacon and set aside. Beat eggs, 1 cup evaporated milk and salt together. Melt butter in skillet and scramble eggs gently until eggs are set. Place half of eggs in a greased 9" x 13" baking dish. Pour half the sauce over the eggs. Spoon on remaining eggs and then remaining sauce. Cover and bake at 300° for 45 to 50 minutes or until heated through. Let stand for 5 minutes before serving. Garnish with parsley. Makes 12 - 16 servings.

CHUCK'S CARAMEL FRENCH TOAST

1 cup packed brown sugar
1/2 cup butter
2 tablespoons light
  corn syrup
12 slices Texas toast
  bread
1/4 cup sugar
1 teaspoon cinnamon,
  divided
6 eggs
1 cup milk
1 teaspoon vanilla

In a small saucepan bring brown sugar, butter and corn syrup to a boil, stirring constantly. Remove from heat and pour into a greased 9" x 13" baking dish. Top with 6 slices of bread. Combine sugar and 1/2 teaspoon cinnamon and sprinkle half over the bread. Place remaining bread on top. Sprinkle with remaining half of cinnamon-sugar and set aside. Beat together eggs, milk, vanilla and remaining 1/2 teaspoon cinnamon. Pour over bread. Cover and chill for 8 hours. Remove from refrigerator 30 minutes before baking. Bake uncovered at 350° for 30 to 35 minutes. Makes 4 - 6 servings.

Recipes From Mountain Meadows Guest Ranch

MANDARIN ORANGE SALAD
WITH RASPBERRY VINAIGRETTE

Baby field greens
Thinly-sliced red onions

1 can mandarin oranges, drained

Vinaigrette Dressing:
2 cups vegetable oil
1/2 cup sugar
2 teaspoons dry mustard
2 teaspoons salt

2/3 cup raspberry vinegar
1 small onion, chopped
2 tablespoons poppy seeds

Make Vinaigrette Dressing by putting all ingredients for it, except poppy seeds, in a blender. Add poppy seeds after dressing is thoroughly blended. Refrigerate until ready to serve. Drizzle on top of arranged greens, onion slices and drained oranges. Makes enough dressing for 12 servings.

PORK TENDERLOIN
WITH APRICOT DIJON SAUCE

1 (4-pound) pork
tenderloin, trimmed
& rubbed with a
mixture of herbs
(rosemary, thyme &
basil), a minced
garlic clove and
1 tablespoon
olive oil

Sauce:
3/4 cup apricot preserves
1/3 cup Dijon mustard
1 1/2 teaspoons
cornstarch
1 1/2 teaspoons Kitchen
Bouquet
1/3 cup soy sauce
3/4 cup water

Marinate the pork in a covered pan overnight or for at least 6 to 8 hours. Roast uncovered at 350° for about 20 to 25 minutes per pound (for about 1 1/2 hours total). Let stand for 10 minutes. Slice diagonally and serve with warm sauce spooned across slices. For Sauce: Combine all ingredients and heat over medium heat, stirring constantly, until sauce thickens and simmers for 1 minute. Makes 8 servings.

Recipes From Mountain Meadows Guest Ranch

UNCLE DAN'S CHEESECAKE

For 1 cheesecake:	For 2 cheesecakes:
1 1/4 pounds cream cheese, softened	2 1/2 pounds cream cheese, softened
1 cup sugar	2 cups sugar
3 eggs	6 eggs
1 tablespoon vanilla	2 tablespoons vanilla

For 1 crust:	
Approximately 2 cups Oreo cookies, crushed	2 tablespoons melted butter

In electric mixer bowl place cream cheese and sugar. Whip at high speed (continually scraping bowl) until very creamy and fluffy, for 3 to 5 minutes. Add eggs and vanilla, beat at high speed until mixture forms firm peaks, for 3 to 5 minutes. It is very hard to overbeat the mixture! Flavor variations: 1 cup chocolate chips, 2 cups butterscotch chips, and/or chocolate syrup or any favorite flavor, Kahlua, Bailey's, etc. Finely crush Oreos in Cuisanart, and mix with melted butter; press into springform pan. Pour cheesecake mixture over crust in pan. Bake at 400° for 20 minutes. Reduce heat to 350° and bake until center doesn't jiggle, for an additional 35 to 60 minutes. Makes 12 servings.

UNCLE DAN'S COOKIES

1 1/2 cups brown sugar	1 teaspoon vanilla
1 stick (1/2 cup) margarine, softened	1 teaspoon salt
	1 teaspoon baking soda
1 stick (1/2 cup) butter, softened	2 1/2 cups all-purpose flour
2 eggs	2 cups chocolate chips
	1 cup nuts (opt.)

In large mixer bowl place brown sugar, margarine, butter, eggs, vanilla, salt and baking soda. Mix at low speed for 1 minute or so. Mix at high speed until mixture forms soft peaks, for 3 to 5 minutes. Add flour and mix at low speed for 1 minute. Stir in chocolate chips and 1 cup nuts, if desired. Drop onto greased cookie sheet (or line pan with baking parchment paper) with 1 ounce scooper. Bake at 350° for 9 1/2 to 10 1/2 minutes, until desired doneness. Cookies will continue to "bake" a little on pan after removal from oven. Makes approximately 2 dozen cookies.

O'Carroll's Bed & Breakfast

5 Paradise Ranch Road • Livingston, MT 59047
406-333-9099 888-577-4420
406-333-9098 FAX
Web site: ocarrollsbandb.com
E-mail: info@ocarrollsbandb.com
Innkeepers: Eleanor Harvey, Dess and Billy Carroll

O'Carroll's B&B is nestled in the heart of beautiful Paradise Valley, 18 miles south of Livingston, MT, on the Yellowstone. There are 5 acres of river front for fishing, launching canoes and float boats, or just relaxing. Each one of our 5 well-appointed guest rooms has its own bath. Our day begins with a Rocky Mountain sunrise, coffee and a full breakfast of fresh fruit or melon, home-baked bread, coffee cake and special egg/meat dishes. (Continental breakfast also available.) With Yellowstone National Park a mere 30-minute drive away, many guests are off to see the scenery and animals: elk, moose, deer, bison, eagles, swans, sheep and if lucky, a black or grizzly bear! Or perhaps a day of fishing, horseback riding, skiing, dog sledding, picnicking, hiking - according to season and visitor's choice. And then at the end of the day, a stunning Rocky Mountain sunset.

Rates: $$$ Includes full/continental breakfast. Children over age 6 are welcome. No pets or smoking, please. We accept MasterCard, Visa and Am Ex.

APPLE & CHEESE BAKE

1 (#2 size) can apples,
  drained
A little less than 1/2
  pound Velveeta cheese

1 stick margarine
1 cup sugar
3/4 cup self-rising
  flour

Drain apples and put in 7" x 11" casserole dish. Microwave Velveeta cheese and margarine until melted. Mix sugar and flour with cheese mixture. Spoon over apples. Bake at 350° for 20 to 25 minutes. Enjoy! Makes approximately 10 - 12 servings.

BARBEQUE BUNS

2 pkgs. yeast
2 cups warm water
  (110° - 130°)
1/4 cup sugar

1 tablespoon salt
1/2 cup butter
5 - 6 cups plain
  flour

Dissolve yeast in bowl with warm water, sugar and salt. Add butter. Stir in flour to make soft dough. Cover and let rise to double. Knead for 8 to 10 minutes. Cover and let rise again. Shape as desired into rolls, buns or individual (small) loaves. Bake at 375° for 15 to 20 minutes. Makes 16 rolls.

DUTCH BABIES WITH FRESH FRUIT JAM

1/3 cup butter
4 eggs
1 cup milk
1 cup flour
1/2 teaspoon baking
  powder
1/2 teaspoon salt

<u>Fresh Fruit Jam</u>:
1 cup hot fresh fruit
  (raspberries,
  blackberries or
  strawberries)
1/2 cup sugar

Put butter in a 3-quart to 4-quart iron skillet and set into a 425° oven. Mix Dutch Baby batter while butter melts. Put eggs in a blender and whirl at high speed for 1 minute. Gradually pour in milk, then slowly add flour. Blend for 30 seconds after adding all flour, baking powder and salt. Pour into hot pan in oven. Bake until puffy and golden brown. Dust with nutmeg. Cut into wedges and serve immediately with Fresh Fruit Jam or syrup. For Jam: Cook hot fresh fruit and sugar until thick. Serve hot. Makes 6 servings.

GOLDEN POTATO CAKES BY DESS

5 cups mashed potatoes
1 stick butter
1/2 cup evaporated milk
1 cup onion, finely
  chopped

1/4 - 1/2 cup cream or
  half and half
2 eggs, beaten
Salt & pepper, to taste
1/2 - 3/4 cup flour

Whip hot potatoes with butter and evaporated milk. Can be done the day before and refrigerated. To the potatoes, add onions, cream, eggs, salt, pepper and flour. Mix well. (Flour is for holding ingredients together. More can be added if necessary.) Cover bottom of frying pan with canola oil. Preheat to medium. Drop spoonfuls (about 2 - 3 tablespoons) of potato mixture into hot oil, cook until golden on each side. Serve hot! Makes 30 - 36 cakes.

HAZELNUT MOCHA MIX

1 (22-ounce) box nonfat dry milk powder
1 (16-ounce) pkg. cane sugar
1 (15-ounce) pkg. chocolate mix for milk (like Nestle's Quik)

1 (11-ounce) jar non-dairy powdered creamer
2 (8-ounce) jars hazelnut non-dairy creamer
1/2 cup cocoa
1/4 cup instant coffee granules

Mix ingredients together. Use 1/4 cup mix to 8 ounces of hot water. (Using hot milk will make a richer beverage.) You can store mixture for up to 3 months.

SOUR CREAM COFFEE CAKE

1 cup butter
2 cups sugar
2 eggs
1 cup sour cream

1/2 teaspoon vanilla
2 cups flour
1 teaspoon baking powder
1/4 teaspoon salt

Tunnel Filling:
4 teaspoons sugar
1 teaspoon cinnamon

1 cup chopped pecans

Cream butter and 2 cups sugar until light and fluffy. Beat in eggs one at a time. Fold in sour cream and vanilla. Combine flour, baking powder and salt by sifting. Fold mixture into egg and sour cream mixture. Place 1/3 batter in greased and floured bundt or tube pan. Combine Filling ingredients. Sprinkle 3/4 of this mixture over batter in pan. Spoon in remaining 2/3 of batter. Sprinkle remaining 1/4 of nut mixture on top. Bake at 350° for one hour or until golden. Cool on rack. Freezes like a dream. Makes 16 servings.

Paradise Gateway Bed & Breakfast

P.O. Box 84 • Emigrant, MT 59027
406-333-4063   800-541-4113
406-333-4626 FAX
Web site: www.wtp.net/go/paradise
E-mail: paradise@gomontana.com
Innkeepers: Pete and Carol Reed

If you've dreamed about a romantic hideaway amid the natural glories of America's Big Sky Country, next to Yellowstone National Park, *Paradise Gateway B&B* is just the place for you. As you eat your hearty gourmet breakfast in this spacious country home on the banks of the Yellowstone River - within view of the breathtaking 10,900 foot tall Emigrant Peak - you'll feel like you're in paradise, indeed. Guests may choose rooms in the Inn or quaint modern log cabins with 100 acres to roam. All with private baths, decorated in French country. A 'cowboy' treat tray is served to guests after a memorable horseback ride or fishing with a top-quality guide in the nation's premier trout waters - the Yellowstone River, which is *Paradise Gateway's* front yard. Guests return frequently as they know they can find the promise of another exciting tomorrow. Our cabin homes are in demand, each on 20 & 30 acres. Very private.

Rates: $$$$ Includes full breakfast. Children are welcome. No pets, please. Restricted smoking (outdoors only). We accept MasterCard and Visa.

BAKED APPLE-ALMOND BREAKFAST PUDDING

5 apples (about 2 pounds) (Golden Delicious, Cortland, McIntosh or Gravenstein) peeled, halved & cored
1 teaspoon vanilla extract
1 cup sugar, divided
2 eggs

1/4 teaspoon almond extract
1/4 teaspoon salt
1 cup flour
1/2 cup unsalted butter, melted
1/2 cup finely chopped, toasted almonds

Preheat oven to 325°. Butter a 2-quart baking dish (such as a round soufflé dish). Peel, halve and core apples. Cut into 1/2" cubes. Place apples in large bowl and toss with vanilla and 2 tablespoons sugar. Spread apples in dish. In small bowl beat remaining sugar with eggs, almond extract, salt, flour and melted butter until smooth. Stir in almonds. Spread batter evenly over fruit. Bake until the top is golden and the apples can be pierced easily with a thin, sharp knife, for 50 to 60 minutes. Serve the pudding warm. Substitute fresh apricots in place of apples for a change. Guests love this dish! Makes 6 servings.

PARMESAN PUFFS

1/4 cup milk
1/4 cup water
1/2 stick unsalted butter (1/4 cup)
1/4 teaspoon salt

1/2 cup flour
2 large eggs
1 cup freshly grated Parmesan cheese
Pepper, to taste

In a heavy saucepan combine milk, water, butter and salt and bring to a boil over high heat. Reduce the heat to moderate, add flour all at once and beat mixture with a wooden spoon until it leaves the side of the pan and forms a ball. Transfer the mixture to a bowl and whisk in eggs, one at a time, whisking well after each addition. Stir in Parmesan cheese and pepper, to taste. Drop the batter in eight mounds on a buttered baking sheet and bake the puffs in upper 1/3 of a preheated 400° oven for 20 minutes until crisp. Guest's favorite!

COFFEE FRAPPÉ

18 - 22 ice cubes,
  crushed
7 fluid ounces double-
  strength coffee, chilled
2 tablespoons granulated
  sugar

2 tablespoons vanilla,
  hazelnut, raspberry or
  other syrup
Whipped cream or ice
  cream, for garnish

Place ice cubes, coffee, sugar and syrup in a blender. Blend until frappé is smooth. Pour into a large, tall glass. Garnish with a dollop of whipped cream or a scoop of your favorite ice cream. Makes 1 (16-ounce) frappé.

PEAR AND HONEY CLAUFOTIS

2 - 3 Bartlett, Anjou or
  Cornice pears (about
  1 pound)
Juice of 1 lime
4 extra large eggs
1/3 cup granulated sugar
2 tablespoons unsalted
  butter, melted

1 cup heavy cream
1 teaspoon ground
  ginger or 1 tablespoon
  chopped candied ginger
Finely julienned zest
  of 1 lime
1/3 cup honey

Preheat oven to 350°. Generously butter a 9" diameter glass or ceramic quiche pan. Place the pan on a heavy duty baking sheet lined with aluminum foil (to protect the oven in case of spills). Peel and core pears and cut them into thin slices. Place pear slices in a small bowl, add lime juice and toss. In a medium bowl whisk together eggs, sugar, butter and cream. Stir in ginger and lime zest. Pour a thin layer of egg mixture into the quiche pan. Drain pear slices and layer them over the egg mixture. Pour in the remaining egg mixture. Dribble honey over the top. Bake until the top is puffed and browned and the filling is set, for 25 to 30 minutes. Serve the Claufotis warm. Makes 6 - 8 servings.

PARADISE GATEWAY SCONES

2 cups white flour
3 tablespoons white sugar
3 1/2 teaspoons baking
  powder
1/4 teaspoon salt
2/3 cup margarine

1/3 cup dried cherries,
  blueberries, dates,
  raisins or cranberries
3/4 cup milk
Additional milk,
  for tops of scones

Sift together flour, sugar, baking powder and salt. Cut in margarine with pastry cutter or fingers until mixture resembles coarse oatmeal. Add fruit and mix together. Add 3/4 cup milk. Mix lightly with a fork until just blended. Add 1 or 2 additional tablespoons of milk, if necessary, to hold mixture together. Preheat oven to 425°. Divide dough into two equal parts and turn on floured board. Pat into circles 1" in thickness. Handle only enough to pat into shape. Score with a knife halfway through to form four portions in each circle. Brush with 1 tablespoon milk. Bake scones for 18 - 20 minutes. Makes 8 scones. Complement with Lemon Curd (see recipe below).

LEMON CURD

3/4 cup sugar
1/2 cup margarine
1/3 cup lemon juice

Grated rind of 2
  lemons
3 eggs, beaten

Place all ingredients in top of double boiler over hot water. Stir until well blended and thick, for about 5 minutes. Stores well in refrigerator. Serve over bread pudding or with scones. Makes 8 - 10 servings. Excellent with Paradise Gateway Scones (see recipe above).

Red Willow Inn

147 West Bridge Road • Hamilton, MT 59840
406-375-1101
Web site: www.redwillowinn.com
E-mail: info@redwillowinn.com
Innkeepers: Susan and John Gudmundsson

Come stay in a beautifully restored piece of the past, built in 1904, and located just one mile from downtown Hamilton. Only 40 miles south of the Missoula International Airport, and easy to find. The beautiful Bitterroot Valley offers lots to do - fishing, hunting, hiking, biking, walks, an 18-hole public golf course, great shopping and restaurants and wonderful weather. We have great decks overlooking the mountains and valley. We offer 3 bedrooms, all with private baths. Includes a healthy, hearty breakfast, inside or outside, overlooking Hamilton. Well worth the visit.

Rates: $$$ Includes full breakfast. No pets, please. Restricted smoking. We accept MasterCard and Visa.

BANANA-STRAWBERRY MORNING SHAKE

1 tablespoon honey
1 banana, cut up
6 - 8 strawberries, cut up
2 tablespoons ground
   flax seed

1 cup whole milk (may
   use skim)
1 cup vanilla yogurt (may
   use fat-free)
3 ice cubes

In blender, blend all ingredients until smooth and pour into glasses. Enjoy! Makes 2 servings.

BLACKBERRY BUTTERMILK COFFEE CAKE

2 cups whole wheat
   pastry flour
2 3/4 cups unbleached
   white flour
1 teaspoon baking powder
1 teaspoon baking soda
1/4 teaspoon sea salt
1 cup butter, softened

1 1/2 cups honey
1 teaspoon vanilla
   extract
4 free range eggs
1 cup buttermilk
2 cups fresh blackberries
   or fresh raspberries
   may be used

Preheat oven to 350°. In medium size bowl combine flours, baking powder, baking soda and salt. In large mixing bowl blend butter and honey with an electric mixer until smooth and creamy. Add vanilla and eggs. Mix well. Add dry ingredients to butter mixture, alternately with buttermilk, until all flour and buttermilk are blended smoothly with the butter mix. Fold in blackberries. Butter a 10" tube pan, pour in batter. Bake for 1 1/4 hours until golden on top and a toothpick comes out clean. Makes 12 servings.

CHEESY ASPARAGUS FRITTATA

2 tablespoons butter
3/4 cup fresh
  asparagus cuts
1 clove, finely chopped
1/4 cup chopped tomato
4 free range eggs

1/4 cup milk
3/4 teaspoon chopped
  fresh chervil leaves
1/8 teaspoon sea salt
1/2 cup shredded Swiss
  or Havarti cheese

Melt butter in 8" ovenproof skillet over medium heat. Cook asparagus with clove for about 3 minutes until crisp-tender. Stir in tomato and reduce heat. Beat eggs, milk, chervil and sea salt until blended. Stir in cheese. Pour over vegetables. Cover and cook for 9 to 11 minutes until eggs are set in center. Remove cover. Set oven to broil, broil frittata about 5" from heat, for about 2 minutes or until top starts to brown. This recipe can be doubled or tripled. Makes 2 servings.

HONEY APPLE-RAISIN BRAN MUFFINS

1/2 cup unbleached flour
3/4 cup whole wheat flour
1/4 cup wheat bran
1 teaspoon baking powder
1 teaspoon ground
  cinnamon
1/3 cup honey

1 free range egg white,
  slightly beaten
1 (8-ounce) carton
  plain yogurt
1/4 cup butter
1/2 cup chopped apples
1/4 cup raisins

In large bowl combine dry ingredients. In small bowl combine wet ingredients. Add wet ingredients to dry until just moistened, then add apples and raisins. Spoon batter into 12 muffin cups coated with oil, filling 3/4 full. Bake at 350° for 18 to 20 minutes until lightly browned. Makes 12 muffins.

MEXICAN STRATA

8 slices whole grain
  bread, crusts removed
1 1/2 cups shredded
  reduced-fat or regular
  cheddar cheese
1 (4-ounce) can chopped
  green chilies, drained

1 (4-ounce) jar
  chopped pimento
1 1/3 cups milk
4 free range eggs
1/4 teaspoon cumin
1 cup salsa
Sour cream, for garnish

Spray an 8" x 8" x 2" baking dish with oil. Remove crust from bread. Place 4 slices of bread in baking dish. Sprinkle with cheese, chilies and pimento. Top with remaining bread. Beat eggs, milk and cumin until blended, pour over bread. Cover and refrigerate for at least 2 hours, but no longer than 24 hours. Heat oven to 325°. Bake for 1 to 1 1/4 hours or until knife inserted in center comes out clean and top is golden brown. Let stand for 10 minutes. Serve with salsa and sour cream. Makes 4 servings.

WHOLE WHEAT HONEY SCONES

3/4 cup whole wheat flour
3/4 cup unbleached flour
1 1/2 teaspoons baking
  powder
1/4 teaspoon baking soda
1/4 teaspoon sea salt

1/4 cup butter
1 large free
  range egg
3/4 cup plain lowfat
  yogurt
1 tablespoon honey

Preheat oven to 400°. Mix dry ingredients in bowl, cut in butter with pastry cutter until mix resembles oatmeal. Add egg, yogurt and honey, mix with fork until dough comes together. Turn dough onto floured surface and knead gently about 8 turns. Roll or pat dough 1" thick. Cut out scones with a 1 1/2" round cutter. Place 1/2" apart on oiled baking sheet. Bake until puffed and golden brown, for 12 to 15 minutes. Cool and serve with homemade jams or marmalade.

The Sanders - Helena's Bed & Breakfast

328 North Ewing • Helena, MT 59601
406-442-3309   406-443-2361 FAX
Web site: www.sandersbb.com
E-mail: thefolks@sandersbb.com
Innkeepers: Rock Ringling and Bobbi Uecker

Nationally acclaimed as one of the 100 best bed and breakfasts in the United States & Canada, *The Sanders* offers elegant accommodations steeped in the history of Montana's capital city. Built in 1875 by Harriet and Wilbur Sanders and restored 112 years later, this historical register home combines the spirit of days gone by with the comforts of today. Seven guest rooms are graced with original furnishings and reflect grand turn-of-the-century living. Each richly detailed room has its own in-room bath, TV, phone and dataport as well as a charming view of Helena and the surrounding valley and mountains. A full breakfast is served each morning in the wainscotted dining room; refreshments await arriving guests each afternoon. Located in the heart of Helena, *The Sanders* is within three blocks of St. Helena's Cathedral, the Original Governor's Mansion, and historic Last Chance Gulch. Also nearby are the State Capitol, the Montana Historical Museum, and fine restaurants and shops.

Rates: $$$ - $$$$ Includes full breakfast. Children are welcome.
No pets or smoking, please. We accept MasterCard, Visa, Am Ex,
Discover and Diners.

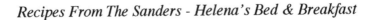

ARTICHOKE AND HAM CASSEROLE

8 hard-boiled eggs, quartered
2 cups diced ham
1 (20-ounce) can artichokes, drained
1/8 cup sauteed onion
1 can cream of mushroom soup
1 can cream of chicken soup
1/4 cup sherry
1 cup shredded cheddar cheese

Boil eggs. Quarter and place on the bottom of a lightly oiled 9" x 13" pan. Layer with ham, artichokes and onion. Mix the soups and sherry. Pour over egg-artichoke layers. Cover with cheese. Bake at 400° for 30 minutes or until cheese is melted. Makes 8 servings.

BREAKFAST PARFAITS À LA SANDERS

Pears, apples, dried cranberries, apricots and fresh fruits, as desired
Yogurt or fruit juice, as desired
Honey or maple syrup (opt.)
Granola and fresh raspberries or blueberries, for garnish

A set of lovely old-fashioned ice cream sundae glasses inspired this *Sanders'* breakfast opener. Exact quantities of fruit and yogurt are determined by the number of servings needed. Combinations of fruit will depend on the season and what you might have in the freezer. Try combining a canned fruit such as apricots with fresh fruits, and experiment with choices of flavored yogurts. Honey or maple syrup can add interest, too. For example, make a fruit salad of pears, apples and dried cranberries, and splash with a bit of orange juice. Set aside for a few minutes so the cranberries begin to soak up the fruit juices. In each sundae glass, start with some of the fruit mix, then a scoop of plain or vanilla yogurt, more fruit, and end with yogurt. Top with a sprinkling of granola and a few fresh raspberries or blueberries.

Recipes From The Sanders - Helena's Bed & Breakfast

CHEDDAR APPLE HARVEST

4 medium baking apples,
  peeled, cored and
  cut into eighths
2 teaspoons fresh
  lemon juice

1/4 cup water
1/4 teaspoon cinnamon
2 tablespoons sugar
1/2 cup shredded
  cheddar cheese

Butter a shallow casserole dish that can be placed in the microwave. Arrange the apple slices in the casserole dish and sprinkle with lemon juice and water. In a small bowl, combine cinnamon and sugar and sprinkle the mixture over the apples. Bake in the microwave oven until the apples are softened, but not mushy. Remove from oven, sprinkle with shredded cheese, then place back in the microwave for a quick moment, just enough to melt the cheese. Serve on individual dessert dishes.

GARDEN FRITTATA

1 red onion, minced
1 red pepper, diced
1 cup sliced mushrooms
  (or any combination of
  available fresh veggies)
1 potato, sliced

Olive oil, for sauteeing
16 eggs
3 tablespoons butter
1/2 cup mozzarella
  cheese, shredded
Parsley, for garnish

Sauté the vegetables in a bit of olive oil, and then fry up the potato. If all this is done the night before, breakfast is a breeze! In the morning, break eggs into a large bowl and whisk lightly. In a large skillet melt butter, then pour in eggs. Cook only until partially set, then cover with sauteed vegetables. Mix lightly. Continue to cook a bit longer, then sprinkle with shredded mozzarella cheese. Now set it under the broiler to melt the cheese. Garnish with parsley. Allow to cool slightly and cut into wedges. Makes 8 servings.

Recipes From The Sanders - Helena's Bed & Breakfast

GERMAN PANCAKE

4 tablespoons butter	1 cup flour
6 eggs	1 cup milk

Heat oven to 400°. Put butter into a 9" x 13" pan and place in oven. Mix eggs, flour and milk together. Pour this mixture into hot butter. Bake until golden brown. Makes 2 - 4 servings.

PETITE SOUFFLÉ

2 eggs, beaten	1 1/2 tablespoons
1 teaspoon water	sour cream
1/2 teaspoon baking	1/2 teaspoon fines herbes
powder	1/2 cup shredded
Tabasco sauce, to taste	cheese

Mix the first six ingredients well, then stir in cheese. Pour into buttered individual soufflé dish. Bake at 350° until set (for about 20 minutes here in Helena, MT). Makes 1 serving.

The Scott Inn Bed & Breakfast

15 West Copper Street • Butte, MT 59701
406-723-7030   800-844-2952
406-782-1415 FAX
Web site: www.butteamerica.com/scott.htm
Innkeepers: Bill and Deb Hands

The Scott Inn is listed on the National Register of Historic Places. It retains the original character of the building when it was built in 1897. Fully restored in 1994, *The Scott Inn* overlooks one of America's largest historic districts. Renovations include seven warm antique-filled rooms, all with private baths, telephones and a quiet common area where you can spend time with our antique books. Enjoy a hearty family-style breakfast, as well as requested intimate dinners in our spacious dining room. *The Scott Inn* is also a convenient base for outdoor fun that can include exploring several ghost towns, horseback riding, rafting trips on the Big Hole River, blue ribbon fishing, spectacular hikes in surrounding mountains, digging for gems in Crystal Park, soaking in a hot spring, skiing at Discovery Basin, or playing golf at the acclaimed Old Works Golf Course. *The Scott Inn* is truly a wonderful place where the "heart can take a breath."

Rates: $$$ Includes full breakfast. Children are welcome. No pets or smoking, please. Limited handicapped access. We accept MasterCard, Visa, Am Ex and Discover.

AUNT PEGGY'S CARAMELS

2 cups sugar
1 1/2 cups Karo light
   corn syrup
1 cup butter, cut into
   small pieces

2 cups evaporated
   milk
2 teaspoons vanilla
2 squares dark chocolate
   (for dark caramels)

Caramelize sugar over medium heat. Add Karo syrup. Cook, stirring constantly, until it's clear. When syrup starts to boil, add butter piece by piece. Add evaporated milk slowly, so as not to stop boiling. Cook to hard ball stage. Add vanilla. Add chocolate, if desired. Pour into greased 9" x 11" glass baking pan or other shallow glass dish. Cool. Cut and wrap. Makes 72 squares.

CALIENTE COCKTAIL

1 small to medium Maui
   gold pineapple, cubed
2 pink grapefruit, 2 navel
   oranges, 2 tangerines,
   1 lime, all supremed
   (save lime zest as
   garnish)

4 ounces mascarpone
   cheese or cream cheese,
   sweetened and thinned
   with 1 - 2 tablespoons
   heavy cream

Simple Syrup:
1/2 jalapeno, seeded &
   chopped

1/3 cup sugar
1/3 cup water
1 tablespoon lime juice

For Simple Syrup: Simmer jalapeno, sugar and water for five minutes or until sugar dissolves. Add lime juice, strain and chill. Combine supremed citric fruits, add to cubed pineapple and marinate with simple syrup for about 10 minutes. Marinating for a longer time will produce a hotter finish. Drain off some of the syrup, dish into wineglasses and top with sweetened, thinned cheese. Garnish with lime zest. Makes 8 servings.

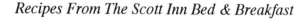

MOM'S APPLE FRITTERS

1/2 cup whole milk or
  buttermilk
2 tablespoons melted
  butter
1 egg
1 cup all-purpose flour
1 teaspoon baking powder

1 tablespoon sugar
1/2 teaspoon salt
1/2 teaspoon apple pie
  spice or cinnamon
2 medium apples (Granny
  Smith or Braeburn)
  peeled, cored & sliced

Beat first three ingredients lightly. Sift together next four ingredients. Add milk mixture to dry ingredients all at once. Add apple pie spice or cinnamon. Stir just enough to mix. Batter should be as thick as heavy cream. Add more milk if necessary. Peel and core apples and slice thin. Dip apple slices in batter. Griddle cook as you would a pancake. Serve with maple syrup or your favorite topping. Enjoy! Makes 4 servings.

SPICED CHERRY BELLS

3 cups flour
1/2 teaspoon baking soda
1/2 teaspoon salt
1 teaspoon ginger
1/2 teaspoon instant
  coffee

1 cup butter
1 1/4 cups firmly packed
  brown sugar
1/4 cup Karo dark
  corn syrup
1 unbeaten egg

Cream Filling:
1/3 cup firmly packed
  brown sugar
1 tablespoon butter

3 tablespoons maraschino
  cherry juice
1 1/2 cups finely chopped
  pecans or walnuts

Mix ingredients for cream filling together. Set aside. Then sift together flour, baking soda, salt, ginger and instant coffee. Cream together 1 cup butter, 1 1/4 cups brown sugar and dark corn syrup. Add egg and 1 teaspoon of cream filling mixture. Add dry ingredients into butter mixture. Mix thoroughly. Roll out dough 1/3 at a time on floured board to 1/8" thickness. Cut into 2 1/2" rounds. Place 1/2 teaspoon cream filling in center of each round. Shape into bell, by folding sides of dough to meet over filling. Make top of bell narrower than "clapper" end. Place a piece of maraschino cherry at wide end of each bell. Bake at 350° for 12 to 15 minutes. Makes 3 dozen cookies.

❖ *Recipes From The Scott Inn Bed & Breakfast*

STAINED GLASS CANDY

3 1/2 cups sugar
1 cup Karo light
  corn syrup
1 cup water

1 teaspoon flavored
  extract (of your choice)
1 (1-ounce) bottle food
  coloring

Combine first three ingredients and cook to 290°. Add flavoring and food coloring. Pour onto cookie sheet dusted with powdered sugar. Cool and break into small "broken glass" size pieces. Makes 50+ pieces of candy.

THE SCOTT INN MULTIGRAIN PILAF OR CEREAL

1/2 cup short-grain
  brown rice
1/2 cup hulled barley
1/2 cup spelt berries
Water, for grains
1 rounded tablespoon
  pine nuts, toasted
2 tablespoons butter

2 teaspoons finely
  diced onion
Zest of 1/4 lemon rind
2 tablespoons currants
Pinch of salt
Pinch of apple pie spice
Fresh ground black
  pepper, to taste

Boil grains together with a little water until crisp, but tender. Drain. Toast pine nuts. Sauté diced onion in butter, with lemon rind and currants. Mix pine nuts, onion and currants into drained grains. Add seasonings, to taste. Serve as pilaf. To use as a breakfast cereal, omit onion, pepper and pine nuts in preparation process. Reheat grains in half and half, with a small amount of brown sugar, and garnish with toasted chopped pecans. Makes 6 servings of pilaf or 3 servings of multigrain cereal.

Thompson Falls Bed & Breakfast

P.O. Box 1903 - 10 Mountain Meadows Lane
Thompson Falls, MT 59873
406-827-0282 (Phone & FAX)
866-FALLSBB (325-5722)
Web site: www.thompsonfallsbnb.net
E-mail: sstoltztfbb@blackfoot.net
Innkeepers: Steve and Terri Stoltz

We are located in Thompson Falls, MT in a spectacular Rocky Mountain setting, on a scenic route to Glacier National Park. A wide variety of activities, including the Clark Fork River, Thompson River, golf course and the Old Jail Museum are available right here. Ski resorts and lakes are close by. Close to Idaho and Spokane, WA. We offer three guest rooms: The Rocky Mountain Room - spacious and bright, with two queen beds and a private bath. The Clark Fork River Room - features rich hues, two queen beds and a full bath which is just across the hall. The Prospect Creek Room - three walls of windows offering views of Big Sky Country, with one full bed, two twin beds and a full bath right out your door. There is a coffee pot, a covered deck with seating, comfortable hammocks in a beautifully-manicured yard and an enclosed game storage area for hunters. Fax machine and internet access available.

Rates: $$ - $$$ Includes full breakfast. Children are welcome. No pets, please. Restricted smoking (outside only). We accept MasterCard and Visa.

BAKED FRENCH TOAST SUPREME

14 slices cinnamon-raisin bread (1" slices)
1/2 cup unsalted butter or margarine, melted
4 whole eggs
2 egg yolks

3/4 cup sugar
3 cups milk
1 cup heavy cream or 4 cups half & half cream
1 tablespoon vanilla
Powdered sugar, to taste

Brush both sides of bread with melted butter and arrange slices evenly in a 9" x 13" buttered pan. In a large bowl beat together whole eggs and egg yolks. Beat in sugar, milk, cream and vanilla. Strain this custard over bread, making sure each slice is evenly moistened. Bake at 350° for 25 minutes or until custard is set and the top is lightly browned. Cool in pan for 15 minutes. Cut into squares. Sprinkle with powdered sugar. Garnish with 3 cups fresh fruit, cut up or 3 cups fresh berries, if desired. Makes about 5 to 7 servings.

FROZEN BREAD SWEET ROLLS

2 loaves frozen bread (thawed in refrigerator)
1 large box vanilla pudding (not instant)
2 tablespoons milk

1/2 cup butter or margarine
1 cup brown sugar
1/2 teaspoon cinnamon

Cook all ingredients, except bread, together to boiling. Break one loaf of bread dough into pieces and cover the bottom of a 9" x 13" pan. Pour boiling mixture over pan, and top with remaining loaf of bread dough, broken into pieces. Let raise for about 2 hours. Bake at 375° for 30 minutes. This can be prepared late at night and put in a cold oven to raise and be baked in the morning. It can also be made in a bundt pan. Makes 8 - 12 servings.

Recipes From Thompson Falls Bed & Breakfast

JACK'S MAD SCRAMBLE

2 tablespoons butter
1 large onion, diced
2 pounds ground beef,
  browned

8 red potatoes, unpeeled
12 large eggs
Grated cheddar cheese
Salt & pepper, to taste

Sauté onion in butter in large skillet. Brown beef in same pan. Wash potatoes, slice with the skins on; add to browned beef and cook. Break eggs into mixture and add cheese. Stir carefully and cook to scramble. Season to taste and serve hot. Makes 8 - 10 servings.

PUMPKIN ORANGE BREAD

1/2 cup shortening
1 1/2 cups sugar
2 eggs
1 cup canned pumpkin
1/2 cup undiluted
  orange juice, divided
1 2/3 cups flour
3/4 teaspoon salt

1/2 teaspoon nutmeg
1/2 teaspoon cloves
1 teaspoon baking soda
1/4 teaspoon baking
  powder
1/2 teaspoon allspice
1/2 cup chopped nuts
1/2 teaspoon cinnamon

Cream shortening and sugar. Add eggs, pumpkin and 1/4 cup orange juice. Beat well. Add dry ingredients and mix well. Bake in greased and floured 9" x 5" pan at 350° for 1 hour. Cool for 5 minutes in pan, then remove. With a toothpick poke small holes in top of loaf. Slowly pour remaining 1/4 cup orange juice over loaf with a teaspoon, allowing juice to be absorbed. Let stand for 1/2 hour before serving or serve cold. Makes 9 - 11 servings.

Recipes From Thompson Falls Bed & Breakfast

PUMPKIN PANCAKES

2 eggs
1 cup milk
1/2 cup cooked pumpkin
1 3/4 cups Bisquick
2 tablespoons sugar

1/2 teaspoon cinnamon
1/2 teaspoon nutmeg
1/2 teaspoon ginger
1/4 cup cooking
  oil

Beat eggs with mixer on high for 5 minutes until thick and lemon-colored. Stir in remaining ingredients. Bake on ungreased griddle until puffed and bubbles begin to break. Turn and bake until golden. Serve with Cider Syrup (recipe below) or your own favorite syrup. Makes 5 dozen 2" pancakes.

CIDER SYRUP

2 tablespoons sugar
2 tablespoons cornstarch
1/2 teaspoon pumpkin
  pie spice

2 cups apple cider
2 tablespoons lemon
  juice
1/4 cup butter

Mix sugar, cornstarch and pumpkin pie spice in pan. Stir in cider and lemon juice. Cook, stirring constantly, until mixture thickens and boils for one minute. Remove from heat and add butter. Pour onto prepared Pumpkin Pancakes (recipe above). Makes 2 - 3 cups syrup.

TIME After TIME Bed & Breakfast

197 Pistol Lane • Victor, MT 59875
406-642-3258
Web site: www.montana.com/timeaftertime
E-mail: timeaftertime@montana.com
Innkeeper: Trish Hatfield

TIME After TIME B&B invites you to experience the beautiful Bitterroot Valley. Spend your leisure time amid spectacular scenery and a million acres of wilderness. Tourist friendly communities offer hiking, hunting, fishing, golfing and biking. Centrally located just 40 minutes from Missoula, the Bitterroot Valley is noted for its fine craftspeople and unique products. Come for the Microbrewery Festival or County Fair, just 8 miles south in Hamilton. You may wish to enjoy the peace and quiet on the 10 acres of secluded park-like grounds. Walk through our woods on picturesque pathways. Birds, deer and wildflowers may be seen among the pines, cottonwoods and aspens. Practice fly-casting on our own small pond or fish the Bitterroot River. *TIME After TIME* offers three spacious and comfortable bed-sitting rooms with private and shared baths. We serve a sumptuous full gourmet breakfast and light refreshments from 4:00 - 5:30 P.M.

Rates: $$ - $$$ Includes full breakfast. Children over age 6 are
welcome. No pets, please. Restricted smoking.
Partial handicapped access.

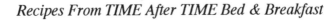

BREAKFAST "SAGED" POTATOES

1/2 - 1 pound ground Italian sausage	1 green bell pepper, chopped
1 medium Walla Walla sweet onion, chopped	1 red or yellow bell pepper, chopped
6 large or 12 small red potatoes, cubed	1 teaspoon rubbed sage
	Salt & pepper, to taste

Brown sausage with chopped onion. Drain. Add cubed potatoes (cut into 1" - 2" cubes). Add chopped peppers (cut into 1" - 2" pieces). Next add sage. Add salt and pepper, to taste. Cover and cook over low heat for approximately 30 minutes. If crisper potatoes are desired, uncover and turn up heat for the last 10 minutes. Makes 6 - 8 servings.

SEAFOOD GIOVANNI

2 large onions, chopped	1 (8-ounce) pkg. vermicelli pasta, cooked
2 bell peppers, chopped	3 cups flaked crabmeat, shrimp or prawns (small)
3 cups fresh mushrooms, sliced	2 cups sour cream
Butter, for sautéing	1 cup grated sharp cheese
3 cups canned tomatoes, drained & chopped	

Sauté onions, bell peppers and mushrooms in butter. Add tomatoes, cooked vermicelli pasta and crabmeat. Mix well. Add sour cream. Mix well again. Turn into greased 9" x 13" casserole. Sprinkle with grated cheese. Bake in moderate oven, at 300° to 350° for 30 minutes. Makes 12 servings.

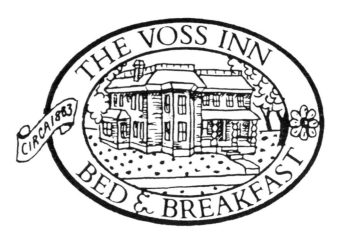

Voss Inn

319 South Willson • Bozeman, MT 59715
406-587-0982 406-585-2964 FAX
Web site: http://www.bozeman-vossinn.com
E-mail: vossinn@imt.net
Innkeepers: Bruce & Frankee Muller

The Voss Inn, built in 1883, is an elegant, brick Victorian with a spacious front porch overlooking an English cottage garden. The entire house is decorated with antiques. All six guest rooms have private baths, some with antique claw-foot tubs, phones and plush terrycloth robes. Guests enjoy a full gourmet breakfast either in the privacy of their rooms or family-style in the guest parlor. The antique radiator bun-warmer is a star attraction of the upstairs buffet area where guests help themselves to an elegant fruit plate, freshly baked muffins or cinnamon rolls, and their choice of a gourmet egg/meat dish served in individual ramekins, freshly made granola or cold cereal. The owners previously operated a photographic safari camp in the African country of Botswana. They continue to enjoy photographing the wildlife of nearby Yellowstone National Park. Special interests include wildlife, fly-fishing, skiing, golf and gourmet cooking - all of which can be enjoyed to the fullest at the *Voss Inn*.

Rates: $$$ - $$$$ Includes full breakfast. Children over age 5 are welcome. No pets or smoking, please. We accept MasterCard, Visa and Am Ex.

Recipe From Voss Inn

CRANBERRY TEA CAKE

2 cups fresh or frozen cranberries
1/2 cup dark brown sugar
1/2 cup finely chopped almonds
2 teaspoons cinnamon
1/4 teaspoon nutmeg
1 tablespoon grated orange zest
2 eggs, beaten
1 cup sour cream

1 1/2 teaspoons vanilla extract
2 1/2 cups cake flour (8.75 ounces)
1 1/4 cups superfine sugar
1/2 teaspoon baking soda
1 teaspoon baking powder
1/2 teaspoon salt
12 tablespoons unsalted butter, softened
Powdered sugar

Preheat oven to 350°. Generously butter a 12-cup bundt pan. Wash and pick over cranberries, and chop coarsely in a food processor in small batches. Mix cranberries in a bowl with brown sugar, almonds, cinnamon, nutmeg and orange zest and set aside. In medium bowl beat together eggs, sour cream and vanilla. In bowl of electric mixer combine next five ingredients (dry ingredients) and mix thoroughly with a wire whisk until well blended. Add softened butter and 1/3 of wet ingredients and mix on low speed until dry ingredients are moistened. Increase speed to medium and beat for 1 1/2 minutes. Scrape down sides of bowl. Add remaining wet ingredients in 3 additions to flour/butter mixture, beating for 20 seconds and scraping down sides of bowl after each addition. Pour half the batter into prepared bundt pan. Spread half the cranberry mixture over top of batter. Pour on remaining batter and sprinkle the rest of cranberry mixture over the top. Bake for 55 to 60 minutes, or until a tester inserted into the center comes out clean. Cool cake in pan on a cooling rack for 10 minutes. Remove cake from pan and cool completely on rack. Sprinkle lightly with powdered sugar.

MAPLE PECAN BRAN MUFFINS

1/3 cup pure maple syrup
1/3 cup butter
20 pecan halves
1 cup natural bran
2/3 cup whole wheat flour
1/2 cup chopped toasted pecans
2 tablespoons firmly packed dark brown sugar

1 1/2 teaspoons minced orange peel
1/2 teaspoon baking soda
1/2 teaspoon baking powder
1/4 teaspoon salt
3/4 cup buttermilk
3 ounces pure maple syrup
1/4 cup (1/2 stick) butter, melted
2 large eggs

Preheat oven to 400°. Generously spray a 12 cup muffin tin with Pam. Melt 1/3 cup maple syrup with 1/3 cup butter in microwave on high until bubbly. Mix well and pour 1 tablespoon of syrup mixture into the bottoms of the prepared muffin cups. Place 2 pecan halves in the bottom of each cup, flat sides up. Set aside. Mix bran and next 7 ingredients in large bowl and stir with a wire whisk to blend. (Be sure to break up all the lumps of brown sugar and orange zest. If you prepare your dry ingredients ahead of time like we do, these lumps will turn to stone!) Whisk buttermilk, 3 ounces maple syrup, 1/4 cup melted butter and eggs in medium bowl. Add this mixture to dry ingredients and mix just until combined. Divide batter evenly among prepared muffin cups filling each to the top. Place pan on a baking sheet and bake until the centers spring back slightly when touched and the tops are nice and golden brown, for about 25 to 30 minutes. (The muffins will overflow slightly.) Cut between muffin edges to separate, if necessary. Immediately invert onto a wire cooling rack. Serve them nice and warm, fresh from the oven! Note: This batter freezes well. Since we don't always know how many people we will have for breakfast at the time we do our prep for the next day, I usually prepare enough dry and wet ingredients for a double batch. The next morning, I bake only what I need and freeze the leftover batter for future use. It freezes quite hard, so it needs to be at least partially defrosted in order to spoon into the muffin tins. Defrost completely before baking. Makes 10 muffins.

VOSS INN TEX-MEX GRITS & EGGS

<u>For Grits</u> - **To make 8 (1/2") slices:**
4 cups milk (lowfat or regular - either is fine)
2 teaspoons salt
1 1/2 cups quick grits
4 tablespoons butter
1 cup pepper jack cheese, grated

4 teaspoons chopped green chilies, or to taste (we use Ortega mild green chilies)
8 large eggs
2 2/3 cups grated pepper jack cheese
4 slices bacon, cooked crisp and crumbled

For grits: Combine milk, salt and grits in 2-quart saucepan. Bring slowly to a boil. Reduce heat to low and cook, stirring constantly, until thick, for about 5 minutes. Remove from heat and stir in butter and 1 cup grated cheese. Beat with electric mixer on medium speed for 5 minutes. Pour grits into 3 (4 1/2" x 3") sterile empty cans and refrigerate overnight. (Since we use quite a bit of corned beef hash, I save the cans and run them through the dishwasher. Removing both the top and bottom of the can makes it easy to push the solid cylinder of grits out in one piece.) Remove grits from cans and wrap tightly until you assemble the egg dishes. Makes enough for about 12 to 14 egg dishes. (Any grits that you do not use can be tightly wrapped and refrigerated for 1 week. Do not freeze. Although I haven't tried to halve the recipe, I see no reason why it wouldn't work.) Preheat oven to 350°. Spray 8 (8-ounce) ramekins with cooking spray. Place 1 (1/2") slice of prepared grits in the bottom of each ramekin. Making a well in the center of grits, top with about 1/2 teaspoon of chopped green chilies (or to taste). Break an egg in the center of the ramekin and top with about 1/3 cup of grated cheese. Sprinkle with crumbled bacon and bake for 20 to 22 minutes, or until egg is set. (For some reason, this particular recipe cooks a little faster than most of the others. I find that the difference between 21 and 23 minutes means a very well-done egg.)

Yellowstone Suites Bed & Breakfast

506 Fourth Street • Gardiner, MT 59030
406-848-7937   800-948-7937
Web site: www.wolftracker.com/ys
E-mail: bandb@gomontana.com
Innkeepers: Anita and John Varley and Vicki LaPlante

Yellowstone Suites, a quaint stone three-story home, is located in a quiet neighborhood by the Yellowstone River. Built in 1904, the house is situated just three blocks from the historic Roosevelt Arch, the original gateway to Yellowstone National Park. Four comfortable rooms, decorated with antiques and historical photographs from the park archives, are arranged for privacy on the second and third floors. Verandahs and peaceful gardens warmly receive you, while a generous resource library and knowledgeable hosts provide windows into Yellowstone's sights, resources and history. Guests can relax in the privacy of their own rooms, in the sitting room, on the covered porch in the garden or on the balcony with a view of the nearby mountains. We serve a full breakfast with a hot dish, muffins, rolls or bagels, hot and cold cereals, yogurt, fresh fruit and a wide choice of beverages.

Rates: $ - $$$ Includes full breakfast. Children are welcome. Pets allowed with prior arrangements. Restricted smoking. We accept MasterCard, Visa, Am Ex and Discover.

CHERRY PUFF PANCAKE

1 tablespoon sugar
2 cups fresh or canned
  sweet cherries,
  drained & pitted
3/4 cup milk
3/4 cup half and half
  cream

3/4 cup flour
2 eggs plus
  1 egg yolk
Pinch of salt
1/4 cup sugar
1 teaspoon vanilla
Powdered sugar, to taste

Preheat oven to 375°. Butter a 10" deep dish pie pan generously and sprinkle with 1 tablespoon sugar. Settle cherries evenly over sugar. In a blender whirl milk, half and half, flour, eggs, egg yolk and salt for 2 minutes. Add 1/4 cup sugar and vanilla and blend. Pour this over cherries. Bake for 45 minutes until puffed and golden. Dust with powdered sugar and serve warm. Makes 5 - 6 servings.

POTPOURRI FRITTATA

6 eggs
1 cup milk
2 tablespoons butter,
  melted
Salt & pepper, to taste
1/2 - 3/4 cup chopped
  vegetables (onion, green
  pepper, mushrooms,
  grated zucchini,
  broccoli, etc.)

1/2 - 3/4 cup cooked,
  crumbled meat (bacon,
  sausage, ham, etc.)
4 ounces grated cheese
  (cheddar, jack, pepper
  jack, etc.)

Preheat oven to 400°. Vigorously whisk or whirl in blender eggs, milk, melted butter and seasonings. Pour into buttered 9" x 9" baking dish. Sprinkle in vegetables (maximum 3/4 cup), meat and cheese. Bake for 20 minutes until set and golden. Makes 6 servings.

Bed & Breakfast Cookbooks from Associations & Individual Inns

American Mornings - Favorite Breakfast Recipes From Bed & Breakfast Inns
Features breakfast recipes & information from 302 inns. 320 pgs. $12.95

Heart Healthy Hospitality - Low Fat Breakfast Recipes / The Manor At Taylor's Store
Features 130 low-fat breakfast recipes. Special lay-flat binding. 160 pgs. $10.95

Mountain Mornings - Breakfasts and other recipes from The Inn at 410 B&B
Features 90 tempting recipes. Special lay-flat binding. 128 pgs. $10.95

What's Cooking Inn Arizona - A Recipe Guidebook of the AZ Assn. of B&B Inns
Features 126 recipes from 21 Arizona inns. 96 pgs. $12.95

Pure Gold - Colorado Treasures / Recipes From B&B Innkeepers of Colorado
Features over 100 recipes from 54 Colorado inns. 96 pgs. $9.95

Colorado Columbine Delicacies - Recipes From B&B Innkeepers of Colorado
Features 115 recipes from 43 Colorado inns. Special lay-flat binding. 112 pgs. $10.95

Inn Good Taste - A Collection of Colorado's Best B&B Recipes
Features 191 recipes from 64 Colorado inns. 176 pgs. $14.95

Inn-describably Delicious - Recipes From The Illinois B&B Assn. Innkeepers
Features recipes from 82 Illinois inns. 112 pgs. $9.95

The Indiana Bed & Breakfast Association Cookbook and Directory
Features recipes from 75 Indiana inns. 96 pgs. $9.95

Hoosier Hospitality - Favorite Recipes from Indiana's Finest B&B Inns
Features over 125 recipes from 54 Indiana inns.   128 pgs. $10.95

Savor the Inns of Kansas - Recipes From Kansas Bed & Breakfasts
Features recipes from 51 Kansas inns. 112 pgs. $9.95

Sunrise To Sunset In Kentucky
Features over 100 recipes from 48 Kentucky inns. 112 pgs. $12.95

Just Inn Time for Breakfast (Michigan Lake To Lake B&B Association)
Features recipes from 93 Michigan inns. Special lay-flat binding. 128 pgs. $10.95

Be Our Guest - Cooking with Missouri's Innkeepers
Features recipes from 43 Missouri inns. 96 pgs. $9.95

A Taste of Montana
Features 84 recipes from 33 Montana inns. 96 pgs. $10.95

Recipes From Big Sky Country - A Collection of Montana's Finest B&B Recipes
Features 139 recipes from 29 Montana inns. 112 pgs. $12.95

Oklahoma Hospitality Innstyle - A Collection of Oklahoma's Finest B&B Recipes
Features over 117 recipes from 25 Oklahoma inns.   96 pgs. $12.95

Palmetto Hospitality - Inn Style (South Carolina)
Features over 90 recipes from 47 South Carolina inns. 112 pgs. $10.00

South Dakota Sunrise - A Collection of Breakfast Recipes
Features 94 recipes from 37 South Dakota inns. 112 pgs. $12.95

Sunrise To Sunset In South Dakota
Features 123 recipes from 27 South Dakota inns. 112 pgs. $12.95

A Taste of Washington State
Features 250 recipes from 83 Washington inns. 192 pgs. $14.95

Another Taste of Washington State
Features 290 recipes from 89 Washington inns. 224 pgs. $15.95

Good Morning West Virginia! - Travel Guide & Recipe Collection
Features 119 recipes from 60 West Virginia inns & travel information. 160 pgs. $12.95

ORDER FORM

To order by phone, please call 800-457-3230.
Visa and MasterCard accepted.

Indicate the quantity of the book(s) that you wish to order below.
Please feel free to copy this form for your order.

MAIL THIS ORDER TO:

Winters Publishing, P.O. Box 501, Greensburg, IN   47240

Quantity

_____	*American Mornings*	$12.95 each _____
_____	*Heart Healthy Hospitality*	$10.95 each _____
_____	*Mountain Mornings*	$10.95 each _____
_____	*What's Cooking Inn Arizona*	$12.95 each _____
_____	*Pure Gold - Colorado Treasures*	$9.95 each _____
_____	*Colorado Columbine Delicacies*	$10.95 each _____
_____	*Inn Good Taste - Colorado*	$14.95 each _____
_____	*Inn-describably Delicious - Illinois*	$9.95 each _____
_____	*Indiana B&B Assn. Cookbook*	$9.95 each _____
_____	*Hoosier Hospitality - Indiana*	$10.95 each _____
_____	*Savor the Inns of Kansas*	$9.95 each _____
_____	*Sunrise To Sunset in Kentucky*	$12.95 each _____
_____	*Just Inn Time for Breakfast - Michigan*	$10.95 each _____
_____	*Be Our Guest - Missouri*	$9.95 each _____
_____	*A Taste of Montana*	$10.95 each _____
_____	*Recipes From Big Sky Country - Montana*	$12.95 each _____
_____	*Oklahoma Hospitality Innstyle*	$12.95 each _____
_____	*Palmetto Hospitality - South Carolina*	$10.00 each _____
_____	*South Dakota Sunrise*	$10.95 each _____
_____	*Sunrise To Sunset In South Dakota*	$12.95 each _____
_____	*A Taste of Washington State*	$14.95 each _____
_____	*Another Taste of Washington State*	$15.95 each _____
_____	*Good Morning West Virginia!*	$12.95 each _____

Shipping Charge $2.00 1st book, $1.00 each additional.   _____

5% Sales Tax (IN residents <u>ONLY</u>)   _____

TOTAL   _____

Send to:

Name: _____

Address: _____

City: _____ State: _____ Zip: _____

Phone: (   ) _____

INDEX OF BED & BREAKFASTS